For Val

I hope you enjoy my book. Thank you for reading. Always forgive!

FORGIVENESS IS FREE

WHY ARE YOU SAVING IT?

APRIL RANDOLPH

All the best,

April Randolph

Copyright © 2019 Alzora Publications
Print Edition

Forgiveness Is Free
By April Randolph

Printed in the United States of America

ISBN 978-1-7343798-0-8

TABLE OF CONTENTS

FORGIVENESS IS FREE

I FORGAVE A cheater, more than once, and we're still married.

Forgiving a cheater is one of the hardest things I've ever done. And it is one of the hardest things you will ever do. But, if you really want it, I'm living proof that you can do it and one day, even trust again.

I've written this book to tell you my story, fully acknowledging the fact that my story and yours are not the same. I know that your situation is entirely, uniquely yours and I don't take lightly any of your story or disregard a moment of your truth.

Though I may not know you, I know we have things in common. I know that your blood is red. I know that you have emotions and feelings, and I know that you, at some point in your life, have or will experience a situation where someone has done you wrong.

Whether it's that guy who cut you off in traffic this morning, or the co-worker that sits next to you, constantly sneezing without covering her mouth, there is someone that has pushed your buttons and possibly pushed you too far.

Or sadly, it's someone closer than that. A loved one, a close friend or perhaps even the person who shares your bed. And you just can't fathom letting them off the hook or allowing them close to your heart again because they just don't deserve it and you don't want them to feel like they've won.

Whatever situation you're struggling to forgive, I hope that you can benefit from my extremely personal story. And I pray that by "putting my business in the street," broken hearts will be mended, marriages will be saved and someone feeling hopeless will find hope.

The road to forgiveness and reconciliation is not easy. There's no cruise control, no spare tire and no Fix-a-Flat on this ride. It's a bumpy, nauseating, turbulent trip and you'll be pumping the brakes the whole way. But, just when you think your engine is dead, along comes this book to give you a jump.

Don't give up yet! There is still hope!

Open your hood, get out your cables, put your foot on the gas and pray. Here comes your roadside assistance.

THE STORM

THE EARLY DAYS

I MET HIM in Rochester, New York, in 1993, when I was 25. I was leaving a company Christmas party with my friend Pat who was driving me home. We stopped at a red light at the corner of Main and St. Paul, and Pat said, "Hey, look at that guy in the car in the next lane. He's staring at you and he's kind of cute."

When I turned to look, a slim, handsome, professional-looking guy was indeed checking me out from the car next to ours. I gave him a smile and he smiled back. I moved my hand in a circular motion, to tell him to roll down his window, and he did. I asked him where he was headed and he said he was following the ladies in the car in front of him, to get something to eat. I had to think fast to make sure that didn't happen.

As the light turned green, I yelled out the window, "Don't follow them, follow us," and he did! We pulled over at the next light and exchanged numbers. And, a few days later, we had our first date. His name was M.

Our first months of dating were magical. He was tall, good-looking and had a great sense of humor. He liked to have fun, and so did I. He had a great job, a good background and he lived in a nice townhome. Nine years my senior and very smart, I spent hours just listening to him talk about anything and everything. I had never met anyone who talked as much as he did, and I still haven't. I hung on to every word. And sometimes I just looked at him while he talked, practicing my first name with his last. Together, they sounded great.

He immediately told me that he had a four-year-old son who lived in another state. He loved him very much. He wanted to be clear that his son came before anything else. T-ball games, birthday celebrations, whatever his son was having, he intended to be a part of it. And he had a very firm rule that his son was not to meet any woman he dated, unless he was seriously involved with her. At that moment I knew he was a keeper and I hoped to meet his son, someday.

We spent nearly every day together, going to movies, concerts and out to dinner. Some entire days were spent at his townhouse, oblivious to the rest of the world. When we went shopping, we held hands and practically skipped down the aisles. Many times, strangers asked, "Are you two in love, or what?" And I'd smile and say "yes" because we were, at least in my mind.

One evening, after an intimate afternoon at his apartment, I went into the bathroom for a shower. While drying off, I noticed something shiny in his garbage can. I pulled the object over the rim and discovered that it was an empty pantyhose package.

Having dressed for work at his place occasionally, it was not unusual for me to place a pantyhose package in the trash. But this brand of hose was not familiar. When I pulled the entire packet from the trash, I noticed that the size was petite and the color was tan. And, as a nearly 6-foot-tall, dark-skinned black woman, this hosiery package was clearly not mine.

I immediately confronted him about the mystery hose and, to my great surprise, he told me that it belonged to his ex-girlfriend. I asked him how his ex's pantyhose package could still be in his garbage, when we'd been dating for months, and he replied, "Well, my ex is not quite my ex, yet."

I discovered that day that not only was there another woman in the picture, but the other woman was, in fact, me.

I couldn't believe he'd been lying to me the whole time. Our perfect love affair had been one-sided. And he didn't even have the decency to say the package belonged to his sister or his mom.

His actual girlfriend was "on her way out," with plans to move to Georgia very soon. And he, not wasting any time, had found her replacement, before she'd even packed up her U-Haul. He was a playboy and I was a fool.

Devastated by the truth, I broke things off with him. He had seemed so nice and so honest and had spent so much time with me that I could hardly believe I was his side chick. I never had a clue.

I ignored his calls for a while. Then one day, because I missed him so much, I decided to let him come over and plead his case. At the advice of my sister, I yelled at him about how hurt I was, throwing plates on the floor for added drama, shattering them to pieces. My sister thought this would be a good tactic to display my pain and brokenness, but she was wrong. All he took from it was that I had lost my mind and should probably be left alone, possibly forever. And all I gained was a pile of broken dinner plates and a huge mess to clean up when he shook his head and walked out the door.

Days passed before he called to ask if we could take a ride together, to talk. He picked me up with a beautiful bouquet of flowers and drove me to Canandaigua Lake where the view was serene and peaceful. As we gazed out at the horizon, he apologized, told me that he was completely done with his girlfriend and asked me to take him back. Then he did the thing that melted me like a slice of cheese on a hot George Foreman Grill…he stood behind me, put his arms around my waist and pulled me close, resting his head on my shoulder.

Now folks, I don't know what that ONE thing is for you, but for me, that was the ONE thing. To me, it was the posture that said, "I'm sorry I hurt you and I won't ever hurt you again," without actually uttering a word. And it got me.

He told me that his now ex-girlfriend knew about us and that she was moving the next day. She had taken a job in Atlanta and was off to start a new life. And in that moment of weakness, that was good enough for me. We started dating again and a few months later, after problems with my landlord, I moved into his townhouse. Surely the world would now know he was all mine. And eventually, to my great pleasure, M took me on the eight-hour drive to meet his son.

His son was a cute little guy who looked just like his mother. And except for the occasional, "I don't have to listen to you; you're not my mom," sass, we got along famously.

M and I happily dated for a couple of years. During that time, we moved out of his townhouse and rented a cute green and white house. It was a quiet place with a bedroom for us and one for his son when he visited, plus a fireplace and a huge kitchen. It was our perfect love nest.

I'd always wanted a dog and that Christmas, my sister gave me a puppy as a present. M had never really had a dog and wasn't sure he wanted one, but the puppy was too cute to let go, so we kept him and named him Cajun. We became a happy little trio.

We spent our weekends taking romantic trips to Toronto and New York City. Plays, festivals, concerts, you name it, and we were there. M's parents lived in Buffalo, an hour away, and the only times we were apart were when M traveled home to visit his mom or to help his dad with a job for his contracting business. Other than that, he was mine.

As time went on and my biological clock ticked louder and louder, I started to become jealous of friends who were getting married. I was nearing 30, after all, and even Pat, who was with me when I met M, had gotten engaged to a man she met on an airplane and was moving away to Florida. And they hadn't even been dating for long.

I dropped dozens of hints that it was time to get married, even suggesting that perhaps I should move out and go back to my ex, if M didn't want me. It was a childish thing to do, but I didn't think so at the time. And then one day I did the ultimate no-no. I gave M an ultimatum. I told him that he had better propose to me by the time Pat got married, or else.

We'd been dating for years, and I felt that the months until Pat's wedding gave him ample time to decide if I was the one for him. Besides, I was a small-town girl from a very religious home, a Christian with leadership responsibilities at church. I was an usher, a choir member and a trustee. How long was I supposed to keep living in sin?

The Engagement

A S DAYS TURNED into weeks and weeks into months, it became painfully clear that getting engaged was not at the forefront of M's mind. Pat's wedding day drew nearer and there was no ring, no proposal and no plan.

On the evening before Pat's wedding, we took the bittersweet trip from New York to Florida for her nuptials. Though excited for her and thrilled to be in her wedding, my heart was torn because it looked as though my day would never come. On the morning of the wedding, as we prepared to leave our hotel for the church, M pulled out a ring, got on his knee and proposed.

And I said, "YES!"

I tried to convince myself that the proposal was from his heart. The ring was perfect, the day was beautiful, but the happiness I had always thought I'd feel when I became engaged, was diminished. I did want to marry him, but with the last-minute-possible proposal and the ultimatum that demanded it, the sentiment did not feel genuine.

We left the hotel and traveled to the church for Pat's wedding in total silence. I stared back and forth from my ring to my now fiancé, wondering what the future held for us.

Pat's wedding was beautiful and I was thrilled for her and her handsome new husband. She had gotten everything she wanted and deserved, and I was up next. My prince had finally proposed.

In an effort to keep the day all about Pat, I hid my ring for hours, feeling like I'd burst from holding in my good news. At the wedding reception, I could hold it no longer. I told Pat I was engaged and showed her my ring. She screamed with glee, took a long look at me, pulled me away from the crowd and said, "You're certainly not excited. Is he?"

I couldn't believe she saw my uneasiness through my happiness, and I wasn't sure of the answer in that moment. M had kept me waiting until the last possible second for a proposal and I wasn't sure that he was certain I was the one for him.

We looked out into the crowd of guests and watched M as he danced with Pat's mom near the pool. He was having a great time, doing the twist and laughing. He had such little rhythm. He smiled at me, winked and looked as happy as I'd ever seen him. A huge sigh of relief flowed through Pat and me and we decided that no one who looked that happy could be unhappy. So, we were pleasantly engaged and life went on.

We set a wedding date that was 18 months out, to save money for a big reception. During those months we set about the busy life of a soon-to-be married couple. In addition to my full-time job, I began working at a library at night to make extra cash for our big day. The 12-hour days were exhausting, but necessary to reach our goal.

Like most brides-to-be, I went shopping with my family to pick out the perfect wedding dress, and we found it very quickly. It was a beautiful gown, made for my exact size, with no adjustments necessary. And every tall woman knows that's a miracle find.

I made appointments with numerous reception halls to find the one that was just right for us. And we visited them all. We decided on a classically rustic facility with old-fashioned carriages adorning the grounds. It was perfect for a small-town girl like me. The invitations were black and white, very polished and pretty, to go with our theme, and our favorite pastor agreed to do the ceremony, which was very important to me. Florists, bakeries, limousine companies, DJs, photographers…you name it, we found it, and it was going to be perfect. M even endured ballroom dance lessons to make me happy. And, like most grooms-to-be, he dutifully came with me to all of the appointments, smiling and showing appropriate interest.

It was an exciting, but challenging time. Balancing two jobs, preparing for a wedding and keeping our love nest in order were draining. Some nights I used the last of my energy to crawl into bed, and some nights, after helping his dad in Buffalo and driving back to Rochester, M would feel just as exhausted. We were tired but our big day was going to be everything I'd ever wanted my wedding to be.

One sunny afternoon, I took Cajun outside for some playtime. The house we rented had a huge backyard and I thought I'd let him get some exercise before I sat down to address the wedding invitations. Our big day was only a few weeks away.

Suddenly, out of nowhere, the sky became dark and rain began pouring from the sky. The wind blew so fiercely that it nearly knocked me off my feet. I grabbed onto a wooden post near the garage to keep my footing. For a moment, the intensity of the storm made us look like Dorothy and Toto from *The Wizard of Oz*. Suddenly afraid, I picked up Cajun and ran to M's truck in the driveway, for shelter.

As branches flew and shutters lost their grip, Cajun and I sat in the truck, waiting out the storm. When the winds died down, I noticed an envelope with M's name on it, lying on the passenger seat. It looked like a fancy party invitation and I thought to myself, "Now, what have we been invited to that he forgot to tell me about?" M was notorious for forgetting to tell me things.

When I picked up the envelope, I noticed that it smelled like perfume. I wondered why it smelled that way.

Then I noticed that it had no return or mailing address on it, which meant that it had been delivered by hand, and only M's name was written on the outside, in cursive.

My curiosity was piqued, so, I opened it and it read:

Dear M,

You are invited to an afternoon of pleasure this Saturday, in Buffalo, at our usual place.

Love, Me

I read the invitation a few times and then placed it down on the seat.

Over and over I recited the words "pleasure," "Buffalo," "our usual place."

Then suddenly, like the sky, my whole world went black.

THE BREAKUP AND BREAKDOWN

I SAT IN the truck for a long time, not wanting to believe what I'd read. One sentence had rushed in like a tsunami and devastated all that I had. My insides felt like screaming but I was not sure I was still breathing. I didn't realize I was crying until I felt Cajun lick the tears from my cheeks.

The rain finally stopped, the skies turned blue, and I sat. Cajun whined to get out of the truck, and I sat. I sat there not knowing what to do or say, unsure if I was capable of moving. I was paralyzed.

A while later, M emerged from the house, wondering where we were. After looking in the garage and searching the backyard, he walked over to the truck, opened the door and said, "Hey. There you are. What are you doing out here?"

I slowly turned to look him in the face, handed him the fancy envelope and watched his expression. He looked at it, gulped like he was swallowing a whole egg, and then looked at the ground. I wanted to watch his face as he read it. He didn't open it because he didn't need to. He now knew that I knew, and the expression of guilt on his face was enough to confirm that my very worst nightmare had indeed come true.

I gasped for just enough air to whisper "Why?" But there was no answer.

I jumped out of the truck, ran inside to the bedroom and wept. My eyes, heart and soul cried until I had no water left to make tears.

When I rose to find tissue for the snot that had encrusted my face, I saw M's wallet on the dresser. I picked it up and slowly went through it, something I had never done before.

In the back of his wallet was a receipt from Victoria's Secret. He had never bought me anything from that store. He had always said that spending money on lingerie was a waste, because lingerie always looked better on the floor. But apparently, it looked good on his other woman, because he had spent his hard-earned money to buy something for her. Money that could have gone towards our wedding fund. The one I worked two jobs for.

I lay back on the bed and cried myself into dry heaves.

Hours later, he came into the bedroom and

asked if I wanted to go for a walk. Not knowing what else to do, I got up, cleaned up my face and walked with him to the park at the end of the street.

Neighbors said hello as we passed and I looked at them like they were aliens, thinking, "How dare they not see that I am not who I used to be. Can't they tell that I'm nothing more than a shell of a person, whose limbs are involuntarily moving down the sidewalk and whose mind is void of brain function, barely alive?" The pain was so overwhelming that I thought that surely, it was easily visible to the world.

When we got to the park, I asked him who she was, and he told me. She was not just some brazen hussy that knew she was messing with an engaged man, but she was someone I knew. Someone who went to the same hairdresser as me, who would sit there and listen to me tell the hairdresser all about my wedding plans.

She was someone he knew before he knew me. I saw him speak to her once at a Juneteenth festival and, when he walked away from her, he commented that she had gained a lot of weight. A comment that made me think she would never be any competition to me.

I asked him how long this had been going on and he had no answer for that.

I told him that since the card was signed "Me," that meant she was special to him. He denied it, but I knew it was true.

I told him that the fact that the hotel was their "usual place" meant this was not a one-time fling. He didn't deny that.

I asked him if their usual place was *our* usual place in Buffalo…the room with the Jacuzzi, near the thruway, and he had no answer for that.

I asked him how he could take ANYONE but me to Buffalo, which is his hometown, where his parents live. And, he had no answer for that.

I asked him if his parents had met her and he shook his head no, and I didn't know whether or not to believe him. After all, they knew we were engaged. Wouldn't they have talked some sense into him? Wouldn't they have told him how stupid he was being?

I knew the answers to all the questions he didn't respond to were very bad. I knew they were devastating, soul-crushing answers.

I asked him how he could cheat on me when we were engaged to be married, and he finally gave me an answer.

He said, "I'm not sure I want to be married. I mean, I love you and all, but I hated the way you forced my hand. I wasn't ready to propose when I did, but I wasn't sure I wanted to lose you, either. I've been looking for weeks for an apartment to move out, because I was going to tell you eventually, and I knew you wouldn't take it well."

And he had never said this to me before then! He had never let on that he was unhappy or unsure. He had made every appointment, told all his friends, everything! He had never said, "I want out!"

And to hear he'd been searching for an apartment to move out was more than I could bear. Why would he be searching for an apartment for himself and planning our wedding at the same time? Why would a person do that?

Why would he be circling apartments and meeting landlords after work, then meet me for appointments with the reception hall, to sample wedding cake and to pick out limousines? What kind of monster would play such games?

And "I knew you wouldn't take it well." Did he really say that? Like this was a totally rational situation and a normal person would look at it and just say, "That's okay."

"I was going to tell you eventually," he said.

Really? Eventually? Our wedding was a few

short weeks away, so…when would eventually be? At the rehearsal dinner?

And the finality of his words… Did they mean he was leaving me? After all, I hadn't even had time to process the betrayal. Wasn't he going to say he was sorry? Wasn't he going to beg me to stay with him and swear he'd never do it again? Didn't he want my forgiveness?

Everything after those words was a blur. The only thing I knew for sure was that he never did say he was sorry. My head was spinning, my heart was exploding and I badly needed to vomit. I sat down on a bench with my head between my legs, trying to fathom the unfathomable.

Moments later, I scraped enough of my dignity off of the pavement to utter the words, "You need to move out, now. I can't stand to look at you."

Then I used the little strength I had left to slowly walk down the street toward our house, which no longer looked like a nest for two lovebirds, but a two-story green and white pile of sticks covered in pigeon poop and maggots.

TRYING TO MOVE ON

H E MOVED OUT pretty quickly. The fact that he had already been looking for a place helped with that. Though I wanted and needed him to leave, I couldn't believe he was actually not fighting to stay. Looking at him before he left was painful. Watching him move out was excruciating.

During those days and for weeks afterward, the light in my eyes did not go back on. All my days were darkness. I can tell you without a doubt that I was not only depressed, but in the midst of a full-blown nervous breakdown. I didn't want to talk to friends or family. I didn't want to see anyone. I wanted to just sit and cry, and so I did. I sat and cried and listened over and over to the music of Anita Baker, who was the only person in the world I cared to hear from.

On the occasions when I had an appetite, I'd drag myself off the couch. Walking was nearly impossible. Every muscle in my body ached and my legs wobbled with each step. And some days, I just sat and drooled. I moved like a 100-year-old woman and felt like I'd aged just as much. I only stopped crying long enough to generate more tears and more energy for crying. And the headaches that come with a good cry were my constant companions.

And the phone calls…those dreaded phone calls. Everyone wanted the remainder of their money. The limousine company, the reception hall…everyone wanted their contract fulfilled and they didn't give a hoot whether an actual wedding took place or not. "A contract is a contract," they said. They didn't care about my broken heart. All they wanted was their cash, and some even threatened to sue me.

As I listened to the threats on my answering machine, I decided it was time to start drinking. But as it turned out, I didn't like the taste of alcohol. I tried beer, wine and several different liquors, but couldn't find anything that tasted tolerable enough to ease the pain. Everything I tried to drink came right back out. I saw it as another cruel twist of fate.

One day, while sitting alone in the dark, I remembered that when M's son last visited us, he mentioned, in all his 6-year-old innocence, that he had met one of Daddy's friends that day and that she was a lady. He told me that she was very nice and, thinking nothing of it because M had many female friends, I gave his son a big hug and never thought about it again.

But in those dark moments, drowning in my self-pity, I remembered. I remembered his son's words and they started to make sense. I realized that M had introduced his son to HER. The nice lady he had met that day was HER.

I remembered how M told me, when we met, that he would never introduce his son to any woman who wasn't important in his life, and yet, he had introduced him to HER. And, because I felt like I was so numb that no more pain could hurt me, I decided to call M and ask him about it, and he, in another sickening moment of truth, confirmed my worst suspicions.

He had actually allowed his son to meet the other woman. His son, who was soon to be MY son. The boy who crawled into my bed when he visited, because he was too scared to sleep during the thunderstorms. The son I cooked dinner for and read stories to at night. The boy who asked to call me Mom. He had introduced our boy to his toy. And worse yet, because he took him to meet HER, that meant she was more than just his toy. That meant he had deep feelings for HER.

The hurt was truly unbearable. The numbness I thought I'd achieved was violently penetrated when this bullet pierced my heart. To this day, more than two decades later, I have nothing to compare it to.

It was about more than the heartbreak of a breakup. It was about the in-your-face betrayal of someone so close. The "smile in your face while sleeping with someone else and looking for an apartment" kind of betrayal. The "trust me while I go out of town for the day to work with my dad, while actually spending the day with my lover" kind of betrayal. The "go ahead and wear yourself out working two jobs to pay for a wedding I don't actually want" kind of betrayal. The "this woman is so important to me that I'm taking my son to meet her" kind of betrayal.

Who does that? How could he injure a faithful heart that way? How could he be that cruel and not ask for forgiveness? Why didn't he beg to stay?

And the nights…those long, quiet nights.

He had always been home at night. Even when he'd been gone for an afternoon tryst, he had always been with me at night. Being alone with the darkness of night brought its own special terrors and pulled me further into despair. Every move of the wind was a tornado to me, surrounding me in a cyclone of sadness. Every creak of the house was a burglar trying to steal what was left of my self-esteem. Each tick of the clock was a moment spent hating the darkness he'd brought to my life, mourning for morning and longing for light.

And the songs… Oh the love songs I played. After wearing out my Anita Baker albums, I had to give others some play.

Every sad song I could think of, I played. And after each one, I played the song for our wedding ballroom dance… "For You," by Kenny Lattimore. The irony was, M wasn't doing anything *for me* anymore. And now that he was gone, I wondered what he was doing *for HER*.

I wondered if he was with her now and if the two of them were laughing at me, calling me stupid for not knowing that they had both made a fool of me. I thought of how much fun they must have, laughing at jokes that were truly on me. I wondered if their sex life was more fun now that they didn't have to worry about getting caught.

Daily, my thoughts wandered to places they

shouldn't go, trudging through an abyss of utter sadness and loneliness, wondering if the next day would seem more worth living.

Thank God I had Cajun…my sweet, loyal puppy to whom I was the most important woman in the world. He gave me reason to get up in the morning, reason to walk outside of the house and the will to go to work each day. After all, he needed to eat, even when I didn't, and because of that, I pulled it together enough to go out and make a living.

On the weekends, I had no hygiene from Friday after work until Monday morning came. There was no reason to wash myself or do my hair. There was nobody to look good for. I didn't want anyone around and I trusted no one. I smelled bad, looked terrible and didn't care at all. But Cajun loved me just the way I was.

There's a scripture that says, "Weeping may stay for the night but rejoicing comes in the morning" (Psalms 30:5). But I didn't feel joy in the mornings. I felt lonely. I missed having M there to greet me at the start of the day. I ran my hand across the sheet on the other side of the bed, and it was flat. There was no heat where his body used to be. I felt only coldness and emptiness.

Sundays were truly my only light. On Sunday, I would turn off my sad love songs to listen to the gospel music on the local radio station WDKX. Listening to gospel had the same effect on my fragile state as the love songs I played. It made me cry. But the gospel music gave me something the love songs didn't…hope. So on Sunday mornings, until noon, WDKX was my second best friend.

One Sunday, I heard a song by a gospel artist named Donnie McClurkin, and it shook me to my core. The song was simply called "Stand." The song was about standing when you're at your lowest point and you don't know what else to do. It was the ultimate encouragement for someone going through a tough time and feeling hopeless. And that someone was me.

The words of that song were the thread to the needle that mended my tattered heart. I played it, I felt it and I became the poster child for it.

I had certainly done all of the crying I could and that had gotten me nowhere. I had certainly prayed for a way to carry on, but hadn't been able to find one. I really didn't know what else to do, except use the little strength I had, to just stand up.

So I stood.

I got up and headed for church, where I hadn't been in weeks.

People were happy to see me. Those who had heard about my breakup were especially kind. They forgave me for not answering their phone calls. The choir sang all of my favorite old songs. And amazingly, after the sermon, the choir sang a new song they'd learned, called "Stand."

So, I went into the church singing "Stand," and I went out of the church singing "Stand." And I decided that was enough confirmation that what I needed to do was keep standing.

So, I stood up and cleaned my house. And I stood up and went to the hairdresser. And I stood up and went shopping for new clothes. And I stood up to depression, stood up to loneliness and stood up for myself. I went to the gym to work out and left a busload of aggression on the treadmill every day. And amazingly, as my body transformed in the mirror and I could actually see myself stronger, I became determined to actually *feel* stronger. So, I returned all the calls I hadn't answered in weeks. I stood up to the people who threatened to sue me and most of them backed down. And I stood up to M and told him that HE, not ME, was going to pay the remaining fees for our reception hall, and he agreed.

Then I dusted off my self-esteem and stood it upright. I read inspiring works like, *Woman, Thou Art Loosed* by T.D. Jakes and all of Joyce Meyer's books, and I covered my bathroom mirror with little notes that let me know I was strong and that God loved me. Each day I added new encouragement like, "Today is the first day of the rest of your life," or, "Be still, and know that I am God," (Psalms 46:10), or "If God brings you to it, He'll bring you through it." And these notes were life-giving to me.

So, I stood up and confided in some good friends and family. I stopped shutting them out and started letting them be who they were…people who cared about me. I let them console me and allowed myself to feel their love. But I was careful not to let my sister talk me into any more events that involved breaking glass.

And I prayed many times, each day. Each time I thought about my pain, I prayed. Whenever my lip began to quiver, I prayed. When I felt myself falling into depression, I prayed. I prayed in church, at home, at work and in the car. I asked God for the strength to stand strong another day and to help me get through each lonely night. And, with Cajun by my side, we stood up to the imaginary noises in the darkness.

I did everything I could think of to rebuild my sanity, and slowly, signs of my former self began to emerge. And, when I'd done all I could...I still stood.

LET THERE BE LIGHT

THINGS STARTED LOOKING a lot brighter when I decided to stand up. I discovered that life looks much better through the lens of a victor than a victim. My heart felt lighter when I realized that having a tragedy in my life didn't mean that my life *was* a tragedy.

M and I were broken up with no plans to reconcile and, as hurt as I was, it was time to move on. So Cajun and I went on with our lives in the house I had shared with M, until I could no longer afford it on my own. I didn't want a roommate, or the memories the house held, so I found a small apartment within walking distance of my job.

Since his love for Cajun was undeniable, M and I eventually shared joint custody of the dog. That's right…joint custody of the dog!

Cajun lived with me during the week and with M on the weekends. Sounds crazy, I'm sure, but it's true.

With my new outlook on life, I was able to

look at M again and eventually become his friend. I could tell he was impressed with how I'd pulled myself together, and I was quite impressed with myself too.

One Friday evening, M stopped by to pick up Cajun for the weekend. His apartment was just a few blocks from mine, so he'd decided to walk over and walk Cajun back to his place. I hugged Cajun goodbye and headed to the hairdresser, excited for a new hairstyle.

An hour later, M walked into the hair salon with a look of sheer horror on his face. I immediately knew something was wrong with my Cajun. With tears in his eyes, he knelt next to the dryer and told me that Cajun had broken loose from his leash, was hit by a car, and died.

My sweet Cajun was dead.

Cajun had been wearing a brand-new collar when M picked him up from my apartment. As they walked to M's place, he jerked to chase after a big dog, which was something he always did, and his new collar came loose. When he was hit, a gentleman who owned a nearby auto shop gave M and Cajun a ride to the animal hospital, but it was too late. My loving puppy who had been my reason for getting up in the morning…was gone.

Because M thought I might want to see him one last time, he'd brought Cajun with him to the salon. I wasn't sure I wanted to see him, but I walked out to the car with M anyway. When I opened the door, there was my puppy, lifeless, lying on a blanket, with rigor mortis setting in.

To add insult to injury, when M called the city to ask what to do with Cajun's body, he was told to just put him on the side of the road. They said that Animal Control would be by to get him, eventually. We were appalled. They told us to discard him like yesterday's trash.

We couldn't do that. So, we found a spot to give him a decent resting place.

Then my life went from mourning to morning to mourning again.

As mad as I was at M for leaving my apartment with Cajun and returning with his lifeless body, I could see that he was clearly upset about his death. In fact, my mother called me that night to tell me that M had called her before coming to the salon. He had been very upset and wanted to know how he could possibly break the news to me that Cajun was dead, after so recently breaking my heart. And since none of my family had spoken to M since our breakup, I knew it took courage for him to call Mom for advice on how to break the awful news to me.

Strangely enough, Cajun's death brought M and me closer. We didn't talk of reconciliation, but the finality of his death was like a line in the sand that said, "Well, the dog is gone. There's no longer an excuse for you to be in each other's presence unless you choose to be. You have to admit you still love each other or walk away…stay in each other's lives, or leave. Now what's it going to be?"

So, we remained in each other's lives, as friends. We'd get together occasionally, talk about everything except who he was dating, and I even watched his apartment for him when he went out of the country on business.

In the meantime, I decided I wanted another dog. A dog all my own.

I went to a local animal shelter and adopted a little Scottie-Poo named Ari. Ari had been in a home where the husband was physically abusing both the wife and dog. The wife had given Ari up for adoption, to save him from her husband. As a result, Ari was very skittish and didn't like a lot of commotion, or men. The vet was quite sure Ari would never do well around children and had no idea how old he was, but guessed he was somewhere between 3 and 5 years old.

He was a bit of a basket case, my Ari, but his eyes lit up when I walked into the room and he jumped and wagged his tail like he had known me all his life. Perhaps he could tell that I had just gotten over being a basket case, myself, and I could relate to him. Whatever the case, we fell in love, so I took the poor little abused dog home so we could shine some light into each other's lives.

Ari and I lived a quiet little life, but he wasn't much of a talker and occasionally, loneliness crept in. I feared being called the "crazy dog lady," so I decided it was time for me to start dating again and I became determined to look more datable. I stopped looking at the ground when I walked down the street and started looking right in the eye of men who looked interesting. And I found it amazing how much more I was noticed when I started noticing others.

I dated a number of guys that year…17 to be exact. I didn't like many of them, but of the couple I did like, there was one in particular named R. He and I would talk for hours on the phone, every night. Many times, we nearly fell asleep because neither of us wanted to hang up. We had the kind of talks you have when you're in love or your relationship is new. He was separated from his wife, who had taken their young child and moved out of state, back home with her parents. We were both in relationship break-up mode.

After long nights of conversation, we still talked each morning. We admitted that we both missed how nice it was to have someone to say "good morning" to. We genuinely liked each other, but knew we were both missing our former loves. We were basically each other's place mats.

One night, after a fun weekend together, R abruptly called to tell me he was going out of town to get his wife back. There was no discussion about it. No apology. No nothing.

A few days later, I called his number and found that he had changed it. I couldn't believe he had really gone that far.

He actually did leave town to reclaim his family, and he returned with his wife and child soon afterward. He called me about a week after their return and asked, "What if I just made the biggest mistake of my life?"

The part of me that was hurt by the suddenness of his resolve to leave me and go reclaim his family wanted to say, "I guess you should have thought about that before you left me to go get her, and changed your phone number," but my better angels respected his need to honor his vows, so instead I replied, "You brought your family back together. How can that be wrong?"

R and I remained friends for years afterward.

As the months passed, I dated a couple more men. I encountered liars, stalkers, men who didn't take care of their children and one who tried to hide the fact that he couldn't read. He was offended when I offered to teach him to read and never called me again. I got over that by telling myself that he probably couldn't read my number.

Dating was horrible and I missed M. We visited each other once or twice a week and the other guys didn't hold a candle to him. He soon found the same was true of me. He wasn't seeing the woman we had broken up over. He said he didn't love her and that his not being ready to marry *me* was never about wanting to be in a relationship with *HER*. Our visits became more frequent, our contact more intimate, and eventually, we became friends with benefits.

And, as sometimes happens to friends with benefits, I became pregnant.

An unplanned pregnancy with a man you were once engaged to, who is currently not even your boyfriend, is a peculiar thing.

M said he was happy about it but I wasn't

quite sure what I should do and was totally unsure what he *really* wanted me to do. And, since our engagement had ended with him looking for his own apartment without even telling me he wasn't ready to get married...how could I trust his reaction to the pregnancy to be a reflection of his true feelings?

A TIME FOR LABOR

WITH A BABY on the way, we decided to move in together again. We found a single house to rent and moved the stuff from his apartment and the stuff from mine into our new home. While it only took me one day to move, it took weeks for M to totally move his stuff in. He really didn't appear to be in a hurry.

Fearing that he might once again be in a situation he was unready for, I spent the first few months of the pregnancy nervous, full of fear and anxiety.

At the beginning of the fifth month, I developed complications. My cervix was too weak to support the baby. I was immediately taken out of work and put on bed rest for the remainder of my pregnancy.

The months on bed rest were terrible. The only time I was able to leave the house was when I went for my weekly doctor appointment. I wasn't even allowed to go to church. I spent each day watching court TV shows, *Oprah* and

The View. And I worried what would become of my poor Ari, because the vet had said he wouldn't be good with kids.

M went to work each day and came home late each evening. He had become very distant while I was on bed rest. He'd take me to the doctor and make sure there was healthy food in the house, but he seemed distracted all the time, like he was just going through the motions. His behavior caused my anxiety to kick into full gear and suspicions took over my thoughts.

To further confirm my bad vibes, I received an envelope in the mail one day, with no return address. Inside was a clipping of a magazine article entitled, "How to Tell if Your Man is Cheating."

I never did confirm who it came from, but it was addressed to me and clearly meant for my eyes. It was obviously intended to give me a heads-up that something very bad was going on. I wondered if it was from HER or from a concerned friend who was aware something was wrong, but afraid to tell me, in my fragile state.

I showed it to M that night and he said, "Who on earth would send you that? Wow! That's crazy!"

When I asked him if he was cheating again, he said, "Of course not!" And that was that. I had no proof otherwise.

When I entered the kitchen one night, M abruptly hung up the phone after checking his work voicemail. He carried an on-call pager at the time, and it was set to go off whenever someone left him a message at work.

For the rest of the night I wondered, "Who is leaving him messages at night and how can I check his voicemail? What would his passcode be? Why is he leaving the room to check it?"

I knew that the standard way to check messages was to call a number and press * to get into the voicemail system, so the next day when he was on his way to work, I called his number several times. I tried out a series of four-digit numbers like his birthday and his son's, hoping one would be the passcode to his voicemail, but none were. Throughout the day, my thoughts were consumed with four-digit numbers that would mean something to him. I sat down to make a list of them when suddenly, a stroke of genius struck my pregnant mama brain.

When M came home that night, I went into the kitchen, out of his sight, and dialed his work phone number. I let it ring long enough for voicemail to pick up and then I hung up the phone. I knew that by activating his voicemail, his pager would sound. So, I went back to sit on the couch.

Moments later, M's pager went off, signaling him to check his work voicemail. He promptly got up and went to the kitchen phone to check it. He looked perplexed at the fact that there was no actual message there, and then sat back down looking confused.

I purposely stayed up later than M that night. When he went to bed, I crept to the kitchen phone and pressed redial. To my great joy, across the caller ID screen came his work phone number and the passcode he used to check the silent voicemail I left earlier. I jumped up as far as my fat feet would take me and said, "Bingo!"

My elation soon turned to fear and I started to tremble inside. Now that I could check his voicemail…what was I going to hear? I knew in my heart that he was keeping something secret and I knew the secret wouldn't be a good one. But, having gone through the trouble to crack the code, how could I not listen? Whatever it was, didn't I deserve to know?

So the next day, when he left for work, I listened to his voicemail messages. There was more than one. They were from a woman. The same woman. HER. The woman he cheated on me with when we were engaged!

Infuriated, I changed my clothes, hopped my 9-month-pregnant self into my car and headed out to his job. When I arrived, I called his desk phone and told him to come out to the parking lot and, when he did, I let him have it!

I told him I knew he was involved with HER again. I screamed at him, told him I hated him, swung at him, spewed every curse word I could think of and got back in the car.

It was quite a spectacle for his co-workers, who heard my screams and watched from the office windows.

As I sped through the parking lot, I watched in the rearview mirror as he ran behind me. I stopped for a moment, thinking, "I should put this car in reverse and run him over!" So I switched the gear from "D" to "R."

Then the baby kicked and I thought of how I'd have to give birth in jail and never see my child. And my better angels helped me take the car out of reverse.

I drove home in tears and when I pulled into the driveway, I sat in the car and wept. I wept for my unborn child who would be born into a broken home. I sat there for hours, wondering what I should do next. I sat there, snorted and cried, until I had to pee.

One thing was for sure…I knew I didn't

want to be home when he got there. And, for a change, I figured he'd be home early to see what my next move was. So, after I used the bathroom, I got back into the car and drove. I drove around trying to figure out where I could go and stay for hours, making him wonder what had become of me. I wanted him to think I had left him or been in an accident. I wanted him to worry where I was, for a change.

The movies seemed like a good way to waste a couple of hours, so I went to a theater and watched a few. Today, I can't even tell you what they were, but I do recall eating two entire buckets of popcorn. When there were no more movies to watch, I went home. When I got there, M was home, sitting in the living room in total silence and darkness. He asked me where I'd been and I gave him a "you deserve to be punched in the mouth for asking me where I've been" glare.

I refused to answer his question, but calmly said, "I don't want you with me when the baby is born. I don't want you anywhere near me."

I told him I didn't know the particulars of what their relationship now entailed, but it really didn't matter. I just wanted him to go away.

M looked at me and, without saying a word, walked upstairs and went to bed. I thought maybe he'd leave the next day, but he didn't leave. He just wouldn't go.

I was nine-months pregnant and, after all those months of bed rest to prevent the baby from arriving early, the baby was late.

For the next week, M was around all the time. There was no working late, no checking his voicemail.

One day I thought to myself, "Now this man has ruined what should have been two of the happiest days of my life…my wedding and the birth of my first child." And I hated him for it.

That day I told him those very words and he looked at me and said nothing. The sight of him made me physically ill, but he still would not go away.

When the big day came, I was frightened to go into labor alone. So, since we had gone to pregnancy classes together, before I went on bed rest, I softened my stance and allowed M in the delivery room.

I have a very high tolerance for physical pain, so labor was quick and easy. M and I slept through most of it, until I was 10 centimeters dilated, when I woke him up and said, "I think I'm ready to push." Then, I pushed a little bit and it was over.

I know that sounds very unusual, because

labor is hard. But I like to think that God thought I'd already had enough pain. So, He gave me a break.

I gave birth to a beautiful daughter that day. M cut the cord and wiped a tear from his eye. And for him and his baby girl, it was love at first sight.

THE LORD AND NANA

S O M AND I set about the business of baby-raising. We continued to live in the same house and never really discussed the voicemails I discovered before the baby's birth. He was almost always around now, except for nights when he worked the late shift. He was a great father and the baby loved her daddy. Diapers and overnight feedings came easy for him. They fell asleep together almost every night with Ari, who, despite the shelter's warning, loved her as much as he loved me.

He was a first-class dad for his girl. He called her Prit, which was short for Pretty, and the name caught on. I soon found myself calling her Prit-Prit and not using her real name at all. Several months later, my mom said the baby wouldn't know her real name if we didn't stop calling her Prit, so we gave her an identity and started using her birth name. But she still remained Prit-Prit in our hearts.

As for the two of us, we were basically

roommates. We were more like a couple of loving parents than a loving couple. But we did love each other and we loved that baby. One day we decided, since we'd tried everything else, that maybe we should try being married. So, we did.

We got married one snowy Thanksgiving weekend. There were no huge plans this time. We had a small wedding and reception with just my sister and his brother as our bridal party. There was no hairdresser or makeup person, no coordinator, no expensive gown or limousine, and we rented the cheapest party house in town for our few guests. We don't even have pictures of the event because our poor photographer died after giving us the proofs, God rest his soul.

M cried when I walked down the aisle. I wasn't sure if they were happy tears or sad, but there were tears. I was purposely late and made him wait at the altar for a few extra minutes…just because.

Things did not get better during the first months of our marriage. Being married didn't make us closer and we were still barely intimate. I hadn't forgotten all of the pain he'd caused or the lies he'd told. The only thing I loved about being married was that we were no longer dating. I didn't trust him at all and the elephant was still in the room, waiting to hit me with its large swinging trunk, ready to crush me at any moment.

Not long after the wedding, I told my grandmother about all of the issues I'd had with M. Like my parents, she lived out of town and wasn't aware of everything that had happened.

Nana was a prayer warrior. Everyone in our family believed that if Nana said it was going to come true, you could bet all the money you had on it. There was no doubt in anyone's mind that Nana had a hotline to God.

To my great relief, when I told her about M's unfaithfulness, Nana told me the story of how my grandfather had cheated on her for years before I was born, and how she'd divorced him because of it. She told me he'd had a whole other life with some woman…a home, a kid and all kinds of joint purchases. He and the other woman had even taken out credit in Nana's name and bought themselves a car.

I was stunned.

My grandfather was a barely functioning alcoholic who lived with us for as long as I could remember, growing up. I'd never known him sober and never known him to have a job. He was the stumbling-all-over-himself kind of drunk. The type you hate to see coming. Nana was forced to be in his presence whenever she visited us, but they never spoke. I had always wondered why she acted as though he was invisible when she came over. Now I understood. He had cheated on her and led a double life for years and she couldn't stand the sight of him.

I'd never known that Nana had experienced such betrayal. It made me wonder if his actions were the reason why he'd become such a drunken, helpless, hopeless soul.

When I asked Nana how she'd managed to move on with her life and find the courage to trust and remarry again, Nana said, "I owe it all to God. There were days when I didn't think I could make it and days when I didn't want to make it. My faith in God helped me see hope, and hope made me feel like things had to get better someday. So, I kept striving towards a better day."

I'd always known Nana as a strong, stern woman who believed in God, but never guessed that her belief in God had helped her survive such trauma and move on to a place of wholeness again. I had no idea what her life was like before she married my step-grandfather, who sadly died of kidney disease a few years after I met M.

When she finished telling me her story, I was still very afraid. I was positive that, with a baby involved, she'd tell me to stay with M. I was sure she'd say we needed to work it out for the sake of the baby. I knew I was about to hear a sermon on how God loves marriage and how M was different than my grandfather. I knew she'd want me to tough it out.

But, to my great surprise, Nana told me that with all M had done to me, it would be okay to leave him. She said his continuous deception was inexcusable and I deserved better. She stopped short of saying that I shouldn't have married him in the first place, but I'm sure she was thinking it…because I certainly was.

I was very relieved to hear her say I should leave him. I began interviewing divorce lawyers, hoping to save up enough money to take the baby and move out.

Though he was present for anything the baby needed, M still seemed distracted when it came to me. And the unmentionable other woman…I knew she was still in the picture. I could feel HER enormous presence.

One day I decided to confirm my suspicions and dial up his voicemail again. When I tried, I discovered he had changed the passcode. It was a smart move, but also reason to believe that, if a change was needed, there was something more to hide. And it made me wonder where he really was on those nights when he worked late.

Then one day I thought of a risky plan to find out if he was still involved with HER.

I had been to M's job many times and knew most of his co-workers, including the security guard at the front desk. That weekend, when M went to help out his dad, I took his work badge off the dresser and drove to his job. Then I walked up to the building, fully prepared to talk up the security guard if I ran into him.

To my great delight, there was no guard at the front desk, so I swiped myself into the building using M's badge and snuck off to his office. Once there, I saw just what I had come for…the voicemail light on his office phone was lit up, with messages waiting.

Since no passcode was needed to check messages from within the office, I pressed the voicemail button and heard, once again, HER voice. And it was clear that they were still spending time together.

I jotted down her phone number from the caller ID and, when the messages were done playing, I snuck back out of the office, past the security desk, and drove back home. I went to bed that night without telling M what I'd done.

The next day, I called HER.

She sounded as if she'd been expecting my call for years. She said she once told M that, if I ever contacted HER, she would tell me the truth. I asked HER what the truth was and she told me.

She said that M came to see HER all the time. He didn't work late nearly as often as he'd said. And sometimes, they met during the day. To prove HER point, she added that two days earlier, when I called M to tell him my uncle died, he was at HER house. Then she went on to tell me the exact outfit he wore the day before that and the day before that. She knew better than I did what my husband had worn to work that week and he'd shared personal information about my family, with HER.

She said she'd told him many times that if he wasn't happy, he should just tell me so. She said she knew he cared for me, but he just didn't seem to want to be committed, to anyone. I asked HER if she was sleeping with my husband and she didn't answer me. Which in itself, was my answer.

She told me she'd do me the favor of letting me tell him that we spoke, and somehow, I believed HER. After all, she was truthful about his visits and she was a faithful person...one who faithfully kept up HER efforts to ruin my relationship with my husband.

Later that day, I confronted M with the phone call I'd had with HER. Since she'd kept her word and not given him a heads-up, he was totally caught off guard. He said he was not in a sexual relationship with her but I didn't believe him and, at that point, really didn't care. I was wise enough by now to not ask for more details, because nothing good would come of them. I was done. I knew enough. I wanted a divorce.

I decided on a divorce lawyer from the list I'd compiled and began the journey of saving money to pay for his fees. It would be a long road, but I felt it would be worth it. I wanted to have him served with papers and not even know it was coming. I couldn't forgive this again.

A few days later, my mother called me at work with an urgent message from Nana. She said, "Nana wanted me to tell you the Lord spoke to her and told her something very important."

Nana had recently been diagnosed with cancer, so I was frightened to hear what came next.

Mom continued, "The Lord told Nana that you need to stay with your husband and that the well-being of your daughter depends on it. You have to work things out!"

I was floored.

I had never heard of the Lord telling anyone something specific like that. I wanted to believe that Nana, nearly 80, was starting to lose it. But, like I said, I'd seen all my life that if Nana said it, that settled it. And Nana had said this awful thing.

I asked Mom to repeat herself. Surely, I'd heard wrong. Nana had said it was okay to leave. How could she just change her mind like that and say that it came from God?

Mom repeated it, word for word, and confirmed the horror that I'd just heard.

I was overwhelmed with anguish and cried each night for a week. Why would God want me to stay, when everything in my being wanted to be done…to walk away…to find someone to love that I could trust.

But Nana had said I should stay.

I was enraged. Why was it okay for her to divorce my grandfather, but not okay for me? I didn't want to stay. I wanted to leave! I had endured enough.

And I was grown; I wasn't a child! This was my life! I didn't have to listen to what my grandmother said. She was old! Maybe she needed a hearing aid before hearing from God.

So, I continued talking to my lawyer, trying to find out how to get the quickest divorce available in New York state. It still required money I didn't yet have.

And all the while a battle raged on in my head. A war Nana's words had sparked. A struggle between my rational mind and her wacky word from God. To forgive or not to forgive…that was the question, and the craziest part was…M hadn't even asked for forgiveness.

Sure, I knew the Bible said to forgive over and over again, but wasn't there some sort of waiver for infidelity? Surely there had to be a grievance process or a probation program or something! There had to be some out! And M had no relationship with God, so shouldn't he be exempt from all of this forgiveness stuff?

And this time we were actually married, legally husband and wife. This was more than a boyfriend-girlfriend thing. We had signed on the dotted line at the courthouse and led the Soul Train line at our reception. We were official!

The battle in my mind was so intense that I told M we needed to talk. I wanted this over and I could no longer wait to serve him papers as a surprise.

So I told M that I wanted out of our marriage and he replied, "No. We have to stay together."

I couldn't understand his response. After all, he was the one who kept tearing us apart.

I told him I didn't believe marriages needed to stay together for the sake of the children and he said he agreed.

I told him I believed children are happiest when they grow up in happy, loving homes, whether with one parent or two. And he agreed with that as well. He reminded me that we both came from divorced homes, and we came out relatively unscathed. I couldn't argue with him there.

I didn't tell M what Nana heard from the Lord, because, at that point, I feared being hurt again more than I feared not doing what the Lord commanded. So, I let him talk on.

He said, "We have to stay together and try to work things out."

"Why on earth should I stay with you?" I screamed. "Now, after all you've put me through…after all the times you've betrayed me for this woman that you can't seem to live without…why do you want to try to work things out with me? What's the point? You're a liar and a cheat and I deserve much better than you!"

Then he looked me straight in the eye and said, "I don't know what's going on, but I had a very strange thing happen to me. I know I sound crazy, but yesterday, when there was no one around, I heard a voice say, 'You need to mend things with your wife. The well-being of your daughter depends on it.' It was weird and I don't know if it was God, or what, but I heard it and I believe it. So, we have to try."

I was shocked.

I looked at him in silence for a moment, trying to read his expression. I was sure, if he were somehow joking, I would be able to tell. After all, I now had plenty of experience discerning when he was up to no good.

But his face didn't change. He didn't flinch. He was sincere and looked a little afraid.

I thought to myself, "Maybe he heard my conversation with Mom. Maybe he knows what Nana heard from the Lord."

Then I remembered that Mom called me at work, and he had no way to know what she'd said. And I had not said a word to anyone about it, because the thought of having to stick things out with him was more than I cared to enunciate.

Now, M was not a Christian and he didn't

come from a family of churchgoers. He didn't know much about the Holy Spirit or hearing from God. So, with the confirmation that he had heard the same thing Nana heard from the Lord, and the look of conviction on his face, I knew he was finally saying something I should actually believe. And so, against all common sense, and completely upset at God for waiting until now to show up, I believed him.

One Step Forward

Now, life wasn't all wine and roses after that. The confirmation of what both Nana and M heard was both astonishing and painful. I prayed they were both wrong. I prayed Nana's hotline to God was full of static the day she heard from the Lord.

I didn't doubt that they were both telling the truth, but the truth was not what I wanted to hear. I still wanted out.

I wanted out so I'd be able to hold my head high with the friends who told me I deserved better and asked me when I was going to wake up.

I wanted out so I could be free to find someone who truly wanted to be with just me.

I wanted out so I could tell my granddaughter how I left a man who continually disrespected me.

I wanted out so I could start a search party to find my long-lost dignity.

But a word from the Lord said we needed to

stay together. And I did not know how I was supposed to do that. I couldn't understand why the Lord was doing all of this talking to folks, but wasn't talking to me. After all, I was the one who'd been betrayed, time and time again. I was the victim here, not them!

My brain flooded with questions I had no answers to and, for days, I wandered blindly through a haze of dismay and confusion. The only thing I knew for certain was that I wanted out and I needed God to want that for me too. So, I interrogated God with the questions that were tormenting my soul.

"Why would you speak to M and not speak to me, God? I was the one who went to church every week, led an auxiliary, sang in the choir and served on the board. Why would you not speak to me?

"And my baby…my precious little girl. Why would you bring her into this mess? Couldn't you just keep her out of it? Our parents were divorced and we came out fine. Why couldn't she be fine too, Lord?"

I simply couldn't understand why God would want me to go through more torture. God who knows every move before it happens…didn't He see more pain in my future? Didn't a child of the Most High deserve better?

Didn't my daughter deserve to grow up with me and a stepdaddy who cherished us both? I was sure I could find someone else to love us.

And what about peace? Didn't I deserve some? After all of the time I'd spent, waiting and wondering where he was…didn't I deserve some peace? Why would the Almighty wish me more sleepless nights?

I'd given up so many things…possible happiness with someone else, my dignity, my pride and my pre-baby figure, to name a few. How would I get those back? Why should I be waiting around for him to hurt me again?

And the biggest question of all surrounded the one thing there was no way to regain…TRUST! How could I ever trust him again and why should I invest in the effort to try?

I lamented over these questions every day. At night, sleep rarely came and, when it did, all my dreams were nightmares. I was constantly running…running with my baby in my arms, panicked and sweating, running for our lives.

I was so conflicted and exhausted from the thoughts racing in my head that I decided to seek counseling. The counselor suggested some readings from wives who'd experienced infidelity and their suggestions for overcoming it. I was astonished to find that people had actually written guides about such a private thing. And their advice was good.

Some suggested that the victim, should he or she decide to stick things out, should now be empowered to ask for what they need. There was a basic consensus that any accommodations, apologies, or changes that the injured spouse requests should be honored by the spouse who engaged in the infidelity as a demonstration that they are truly interested in repairing the relationship. This referred to requests within reason, of course. Things like castration were not an option.

I told M about these findings and, to my surprise, he asked, "What do you want me to do to prove to you that I want to make things right? Tell me. I'll do it."

I looked at him and replied, "I'll let you know."

Then I turned and walked away, thinking, "I'd really like you to get hit by a bus, but I don't have any life insurance on you right now, so it can wait."

I still loved him, but also hated him, and I really just wanted out. I was so mad at him and God, but especially God. How could He want me to stay with this man, but not tell me how? I was determined to stay in God's face until he got tired of me asking, so I kept going to church to let God know that He owed me some answers. And when I couldn't talk to God out loud at work, I'd occasionally look towards the sky and give Him the stink eye, to let Him know I was still mad and still waiting for a response.

One night at a church team meeting, the ladies were discussing a class at another local church, a class I had previously taken, called Understanding God's Word. Their discussion reminded me of how powerful the class had been and what a great resource it was for new and mature Christians alike. The class met weekly for several months, culminating in water baptism, for those who completed the course and were interested. There was plenty of homework and tests along the way and it covered topics from salvation to fruits of the spirit and speaking in tongues, right down to a foot-washing service. And, as the ladies talked on, it hit me. I knew what M had to do if I were ever to consider trusting him again. More so than a relationship with me, he needed to build a relationship with God.

So I told him he'd need to take the Understanding God's Word class for several months, without quitting, and he told me he would. Then he signed up. And although I'd already taken the singles version of the class, I took the couples version with him. That way, I was able to see what God's word said specifically for couples and, as an added bonus, be sure he was actually showing up for class each night.

Participating in that class was life-changing for M. When he was a child, his parents didn't attend church regularly, but believed in God, so they occasionally sent him to church with other family members. And, except for escorting me and the baby to church, he had never purposely sought out the presence of God.

The class taught M all about who God is and, the more he learned, the more interested he became. One of the most important things he learned about was humility. He discovered that his success in life was not of his own doing and that he owed everything he had…his intelligence, job, good looks, children, money, wife…everything he prided himself on, to God (James 1:17). He learned that there was a higher power that knew him before he was born (Jeremiah 1:5), was with him every day (Psalms 73:23), and knew the innermost thoughts of his heart (Hebrews 4:12). He discovered what it meant to be a double-minded man (James 1:8), and he learned that he had found a good thing in finding me (Proverbs 18:22). He learned about mercy, grace and forgiveness (Nehemiah 9:17), and began to realize how blessed he was for all the grace and forgiveness he'd been granted throughout his life.

I could see the change in him as the months passed. He was becoming a new person and a better one. At the end of the course, he was baptized. I cried when he came up out of the water and so did our special guest from out of town…my nana.

I was thrilled that M was now saved, but his becoming saved changed him far more than it changed me. I hoped that now that he had a relationship with God, he would surely have second thoughts if he was about to cheat. I thought that now he'd have a conscience when he did wrong, or maybe he'd be worried that an omnipotent God was reading his thoughts as he contemplated contacting her. After all, Proverbs 5:21 says, "For your ways are in full view of the Lord, and he examines all your paths."

I was very proud of M and how far he'd come, but I still didn't trust him at all.

THE ANGER

A S THE YEARS went on, so did our lives. I discovered that some things were easier being married, which made life quite convenient. I no longer had to introduce M to people as my boyfriend, our daughter had his name and I had a date to wherever I wanted to go.

We were a cute couple on the outside, but on the inside, I still really despised him.

Each day I prayed that a mystery check would show up in the mail and would contain enough money for me to move far away, purchase a house and a divorce. I crossed off each day on the calendar as one more day towards our daughter being grown up…one more day towards freedom.

M continued to grow in his relationship with God, long after graduating from class, and really sought after His presence in his life. He attended church regularly and volunteered wherever and whenever he was needed. And most things I requested of him, he did. But like all couples, we had our fights.

M had a habit of saying, "I'll call you back later," and not calling at all, or of saying, "I'll be home in 10 minutes," and showing up an hour later. This wasn't just something he did with me, but with everyone. It was something he was well-known for.

In fact, one day his work team made a video about their services and at the end of the video, they rolled the credits of each person on the team. After all of his co-workers' names scrolled quickly across the screen, there was an intentional 10-second pause, with darkness, before M's name made an appearance, very late and alone. It was his team's lighthearted way of letting him know that he's always late and folks are always waiting for him to show up.

This tendency to tardiness led to many, many disagreements between us as I oftentimes found myself late to things that were very important to me. And it was extremely difficult for a person who was tasked with trusting the untrustable to be comfortable with why the untrustable wasn't where they said they would be, when they said they would be.

Each time this happened, it justified my loathing of his presence. I felt disrespected and disregarded, and I determined that there should be no intimacy in our marriage, because he didn't deserve any. I didn't talk to him much and when I did, my tone was sharp. There was no closeness, no sharing. I was married and lonely. And I still wanted out.

So I started confiding my discontent in my old friend R, the one who reclaimed his wife and child when M and I were broken up. I told him all of my woes and he listened, and I did the same for him. When M made me angry, I called R. When M seemed distracted, I called R. Even when M was spending what I thought was too much time volunteering at church, I called R. Any excuse would do. I was totally hooked on talking to R, and our relationship, unlike before, was nonsexual. He insisted he was happily married, but there wasn't a day that passed where we didn't talk by phone or email, and our conversations were very deep.

I felt a huge satisfaction from my conversations with R, behind M's back. I felt justified and vindicated. It was as if my time had finally come to be the keeper of secrets. I was now the one with the power to hurt or punish, the one with the upper hand. And I believed that even if M were still cheating on me, I'd be okay. I was confident that, at any moment I chose, I could do the same and he'd have no right to complain.

My talks and visits with R continued for months and, during that time, my marriage stayed the same. There were lots of good times with our girl, but rare intimacy, little interaction and no conversation on how to make things better. But the one thing that continued to improve was M's relationship with God. It grew stronger and more mature each day. And deep in my heart, I resented him for waiting until our relationship was ruined to become a Christian.

One day R and I met at one of our meeting spots to chat, and he asked me if I thought he and I were having an affair. My reply was, "Of course not; we're not even having sex."

Then he asked if I'd be able to go home and tell M that we had been together that day, and I again replied, "Of course I could. And if I did, he'd have no right to complain."

Then he asked me my thoughts on emotional affairs…where two people are attracted to but not sexually involved with one another, but care deeply for one another and desire to see or speak to each other every day.

I stared at R for a while, then I told him that I thought emotional affairs were wrong.

He stared back at me with a devilish smile and replied, "Really?" And I remembered that devilish smile from the days before his wife came back. I remembered it was the gateway to all kinds of unholy acts.

Then he asked me if an emotional affair was somehow less serious than a sexual one, and I said, "I don't really know."

Then he said, "Men are sexual beings who often have sex for the sake of physical gratification, but when women have sex, it is usually tied to emotion. A man can have sex with a woman and not feel tied to her at all, but it's different for women. It's much easier for a woman to capture a man's private part, than his heart. So, when you've captured a man's heart, the seriousness of the relationship goes to a whole new level. And, since most women would rather have a man who loves them than a man who only wants to have sex with them, wouldn't a marriage be in more danger if a spouse was having an emotional affair than a physical one? After all, the cheated spouse would be in danger of losing her mate's heart."

I didn't know exactly where R was going with this, but I had an idea, and I told him he had a good point. Then he stared at me again, with the same devilish smile, and asked, "So, now do you think we're having an affair?"

R and I sat and looked at each other for a long time. He still had the devilish smile on his face. I wondered how someone could smile for that long without their cheeks hurting. We sat there not speaking, until it started to become dark and, in an effort to break the intensity, I said, "We'd better get going, it's getting late and we need to get home."

That night I thought long and hard about R's question. I truly felt that M had no right to complain about my relationship with R. It was nonsexual and a payback, of sorts. But R's wife…his poor unsuspecting wife who had no idea I existed, deserved better.

I was unsure if R was trying to say that we were having an emotional affair…or if he was trying to tell me we might as well have a sexual one…or if he was trying to tell me I had stolen his heart, or all of the above, but I thought it was best that we both seriously consider what he had said.

As Christians, we both knew that Matthew 5:28 says, "Anyone who even looks at a woman with lust has already committed adultery with her in his heart." And we knew that an attraction existed between us, so we agreed to call it quits and go about the business of working on our marriages, without the advice and intervention of the other.

I missed having R as a sounding board, but

with each day that passed, it got easier.

Soon after, M and I decided to join a new church and selected one near our home. As we made friends with other couples and became involved in ministry, I thought, "These poor people have no idea who they're dealing with. The two of us are a mess!"

At church marriage conferences, when asked what we loved most about each other, we always gave the same response. M's was, "She keeps me focused," and mine was, "He's a great father."

By "focused," M didn't mean he only had eyes for me, he meant I reminded him of events and appointments. And I meant it when I said he was a great father. But as we sat and watched other couples profess their undying love for one another, this was the best we could do. *Focus* and *fatherhood*. We had nothing lovey-dovey to say and no praise about how we made each other happy. His infidelity had ruined that. So, I listened to the other couples' love stories and continued my prayer that freedom was on its way.

And freedom did come, but not the way I expected.

One bitter April morning, right before my birthday, God dispatched his very best angels to earth, to give Nana her wings. She lost her fight to breast cancer, which had come and gone and come again, spreading quickly throughout her body.

Before she was terminally ill, Nana met a nice man in his 70s, named Ron, who really took a liking to her. And, though she wouldn't admit it, she was in love. When she became bedridden, she didn't want to see him, because she didn't want him to see her incapacitated. But one day, after many unanswered phone messages, Ron showed up at her house and asked us to tell her he was there.

We told him that she wasn't up to seeing visitors, but he insisted that he see her and said he wouldn't leave until he did.

We weren't sure what to do, because we liked Ron and didn't want to call the police, but Nana had barely moved in days, except for labored breathing. We knew she loved Ron though, and his refusal to leave meant he loved her too, so we decided to let him see her, before she passed.

Despite being on morphine and near death, when we told Nana that Ron was in the living room, she got out of bed, put on a wig and a dress and walked out into the living room like she was perfectly healthy.

We stared at her in wonder and watched as she entertained her company, like any other day, having tea, laughing and watching TV. When she died a few days later, Ron said, "I didn't even know she was that sick."

Isn't it something…what love will do?

As the cancer affected her brain and her memory became scarce those last few days, Nana would shout, "Lord, I know you hear me," and, "Thank you, Jesus," throughout the day. And I believe, just as clearly as she heard the words God gave her for my marriage, God heard the prayer of his good and faithful servant and decided to set my nana free.

THE BITTERNESS

WITH NANA'S DEATH came a new conflict to resolve. Now that she was gone, would it be okay if I left my husband? The fact that she would not be alive to see my marriage crumble meant I could finally do what I wanted.

I toyed with the thought of leaving and getting a divorce, but since my miracle check—the one that would give me enough money for a divorce, a house and no worries—had yet to arrive, my leaving would still have to wait. And deep down inside, I knew in my heart that God's word had no deadline and His promises didn't end with her death.

So we stayed together, enjoying our parenting life and, as time went on, enjoying each other occasionally. I was in my mid-30s then and we knew, if more children were in our future, we'd have to start making that happen. So more intimacy returned to our marriage and we gave birth to our son—a gorgeous, bright-eyed, inquisitive little boy who brought happy distractions to our unhappy marriage.

Our daughter had troubles in school, both behavioral and educational, that caused us to communicate more frequently and with purpose. We couldn't understand why she struggled to learn and it grieved us deeply. We prayed together for our children and occasionally went on date nights, but things were still not right. We were not the happy couple we appeared to be and, finally, we decided to seek help.

As I sought out a counselor, I purposely looked for a male. I felt that M would be more comfortable with a male and that, if a male were to tell him how horribly he'd treated me, he would surely feel like the jerk that he was. I thought hearing it from a woman would somehow hold less weight. I knew we would need many sessions, which would cost a lot, so we settled for a male counselor named Jim who was referred to us by my Employee Assistance Program for six months of therapy.

Each week we met with Jim and, as usual, M was late for every appointment. Jim commented on M's tardiness a couple of times, but it didn't make a difference to M. It was who he was.

In one-hour increments over a course of months, I told Jim all about my relationship with M. I told him about the cheating and the lies that accompanied it. I told him about how inconsiderate M was with his time. I told him how hard it was to trust M when he traveled to Buffalo to help his parents. And to make matters worse, M's dad had become sick and M had taken over his business, causing him to travel to Buffalo multiple times per week.

I told Jim about all the nights I'd wait up and worry, not knowing if he was dead or alive. And I told him that my dislike of my husband grew each time he forgot something, broke something, missed something or didn't do something he said he would do.

And each week I listened as M told his side of the story…how he wasn't ready to live with me when I moved in with him in the first place…how he didn't like the fact that I gave him an ultimatum for proposing to me…how he loved Cajun, but didn't like the fact that I accepted a dog without his permission and, most of all…how he didn't like it that I was mad all the time.

None of these things were a surprise to me, but they vexed me, nonetheless, except for the fact that he didn't like me being mad. When I was mad it was for a good reason. And, despite anything I'd done that he didn't like, his cheating trumped all!

Week after week we left counseling feeling defeated. Talking about past hurts was both painful and exhausting and it brought about feelings I'd tried to bury in a place where they'd never resurface. Many times, I considered not going back.

One day, Jim decided to stop listening and nodding and actually start giving advice. He asked me if I'd forgiven M for his indiscretions and I told him that I wouldn't still be with M if I hadn't forgiven him. He asked me why I worried about M when he went out of town to visit his parents. I told him it worried me because M would say he'd be home at 10, but not return until after midnight or 1 a.m. I told him it was inconsiderate because I'd sit up, worried he had been in an accident, and he didn't have the decency to call. And I told him that Buffalo was where he'd go to have trysts with his little concubine.

Then Jim asked me if I was a person of faith, which was strange, because Jim wasn't.

I told him that I was and he responded, "If you are a person of faith, then where is your faith? If you believe in God and pray to Him for your husband's safe travels, then why are you staying up and worrying?"

The score was Jim 1, me zero.

When I reminded Jim that the main reason I hated M's trips to Buffalo was the fact that he'd cheated on me there, Jim replied, "If you've truly forgiven him, you'll have to find a way to get over Buffalo. Either that, or you can ask him to never visit his parents again. It's your choice."

Jim struck a low blow with that one, but I had to give him the point. Jim 2, me still zero.

I left that visit praying that God would send me enough money to see a counselor other than Jim.

The miracle check didn't arrive, so the following week, we returned to Jim's office. This time Jim seemed more on my side. He zinged M in the same way he had stung me the week before. He asked M questions like, "If you consider yourself a person of integrity, then why don't you keep your word?" and, "Why do you seldom tell people what you really feel, instead of acting out on feelings you haven't verbally expressed?"

M didn't have good answers to these questions and I loved it! I could tell he was very annoyed by them and I thought they were wonderful!

Jim interrogated M that way for the next

couple of visits. He told M he was passive-aggressive and prompted me to look it up. I did so, agreed with his assessment and began to like Jim again. He had given me insight into something about M that I had never been able to put a name to.

After our visits, M and I were short with each other at home. It seemed as if one of us always left counseling with the short end of the stick, the most blame, the most shame. One of us always felt more "right." One night, tired of the new arguments that the old pain brought about, I screamed the words I had longed to say: "I just want you to leave!"

I told M to get out and I meant it. I wanted him out of my life. I promised him that as long as we both prayed for our daughter, she would be fine, and I believed it. I knew he had to be just as tired as I was of trying to make things work. I was giving him an out. Giving us an out.

But, as usual, M wouldn't leave. He told me that if he left, he wouldn't come back, and I told him I'd appreciate that.

But he still didn't leave. No matter how cold I was, he just wouldn't leave!

And so, our counseling, like our misery, continued.

We began to have one-on-one visits with

Jim, which were awkward because we weren't able to hear what we were saying about one another.

During one of my visits alone, Jim asked me again if I'd forgiven M for his infidelity, and I told him I had.

He then asked me if I thought M was still cheating on me and I told him that I didn't, which was true. I really hadn't suspected M of cheating since he'd gotten to know the Lord and, more importantly, I no longer sensed HER presence in our lives. It seemed one positive that had come out of all of my pain was that I had developed a very keen spirit of discernment.

Then Jim asked me to define forgiveness, as I believed it to be. I did so, citing scriptures and examples. I told him that forgiveness sets the person who was wronged, free. I cited the analogy of how harboring unforgiveness is like taking poison and expecting the person who wronged you to die. I told him that God's word says we are to always forgive. I told him about all of the benefits of forgiveness and how I believed firmly in it.

Then Jim asked, **"How can this wonderful forgiveness you describe coexist with the bitterness you hold against your husband? Have you considered that perhaps M still**

does things that make you angry because he feels there's nothing he can do to make you happy…nothing he can do to ease your bitterness…nothing he can do to earn the forgiveness you preach, but, according to your description, aren't practicing?"

In short, Jim called me a hypocrite.

I glared at him from across the room. The anger I'd felt towards my husband for years was nothing compared to the fury I felt for Jim at that moment. **The nerve of him…to question me about forgiveness…to call me bitter!** What kind of counselor was he? Could he not see that I was the victim here? Had he not been listening all these weeks? Didn't he know I had a right to my anger?

Then Jim asked me, "When you pray for your marriage, what exactly do you pray for?"

His question broke the death stare in my eyes, which obviously didn't work on him because he was still breathing. My blood began circulating again. I wanted to tell him that I prayed my marriage would be loving and long-lasting and that I prayed we'd be together forever. I wanted to say something to defend myself from where I knew he was going with this question, but I felt he already knew the answer. I felt he already knew that I prayed *about* my marriage, but never *for* my marriage.

Then, to my great pleasure, the bell rang, signaling that Jim's next patient had arrived, so I gathered my things, said goodbye and sped out the door.

Our next meeting with Jim was the last one covered by the Employee Assistance Program and it was short and to the point. Jim summed up our time together and where we stood at that moment. He told us that he really couldn't come up with enough reasons for us to stay together. He said we were both very likable people, but both very stubborn. His parting words to us were, "Sometimes two really nice people just don't belong together. It's sad but it happens. Good luck to you both!"

And with that, Jim sent us out into the world to fend for our marriage, alone.

A New Season

I couldn't believe Jim left us that way. It seemed we were just as broken in the end as we were in the beginning. And he didn't seem to care. There were no words of wisdom and no offer to continue our counseling if we paid out of pocket. No advice on how to move forward and no hope. Where was our patient care plan?

Ironically, as divisive as it was, "Sometimes two really nice people just don't belong together," became a rallying cry for M and me. It became a challenge of sorts.

We really were two very nice people, but who was Jim to suggest we didn't belong together? After all, we had bared our souls to him. We had told him the good, the bad and the ugly and we were still together. We were a force to be reckoned with. We had weathered the storm.

So, we set out on a mission to prove Jim wrong. Since neither of us really liked him in the first place and he'd brought us more arguments than solutions, we decided Jim was a quack.

I became determined to prove I wasn't a hypocrite. I couldn't deny the bitterness I'd held in my heart for years, but I could change it. I could stop treating M badly, stop criticizing, and stop blaming. I could stop letting our past steal our future.

So, for the first time in years, I tried being nice to M.

I asked about his day and listened for his response. I greeted him with a kiss when he came home from work. I didn't tense up when he told me he was going to Buffalo and I didn't jump down his throat when he was later than expected. And I began to give him a grace period. I accepted that 6:00 to the universe meant 7:00 to M, and I started planning life accordingly.

And gradually, things changed.

With each act of kindness, consideration and respect that I showed to M, he responded with the same in return. He smiled at each smile and returned each hug using every muscle in his body.

And he started being considerate.

He began being late less often and when he couldn't avoid it, he called. He put thought into gifts and planned anniversary trips. He helped more around the house and took on more homework duty. He helped with math and science and I took English and social studies.

The changes in our lives were wonderful and touched me in a way I no longer thought was possible. We were fighting together for something other than our children, for a change. We were fighting together for us. And for the first time since he and I became "us," I was grateful.

One night before bed, I thought about just how far we'd come and I kneeled to thank God for the progress. And as I'd been doing since our time with Jim, I prayed not just for my husband, but FOR our marriage.

For years I had prayed for his safety because I didn't want my children to be without their dad. For years I had prayed over his job, because we were a two-income family. For years I had prayed for his family, because he loved them, a lot. But the truth was, until then, I had not really prayed *for* our marriage. I had heard about it, went to conferences about it and told others to do it, but the bitterness I'd harbored in my heart had kept me from praying for God to save our marriage.

I remembered the countless times I had prayed that M would go away…the nights I cried out to God to get me out of our marriage and the hopes I had placed on the check that would come in the mail. The miracle check that would unseal my anguish, quiet my rage and set my broken heart free.

But everything changed when I changed my prayer.

I asked God to forgive my ungratefulness. He had changed my husband into a man who sought after God, but I, in all of my selfishness and unforgiveness, had shown no appreciation for the gift God had given me.

I had spent so many years continuing to be the victim, that I'd completely overlooked the victory.

So, I prayed for my marriage and thanked God that we were still together. I thanked him that my husband didn't leave any of the times I'd asked him to. I praised Him for the word He had given to Nana and M, and I thanked him for a quack named Jim.

The more I prayed for my marriage, the more God revealed to me. The first thing I clearly needed to work on was our intimacy. I needed to initiate it and I needed to enjoy it. I worked hard at that and, with our improved relationship, intimacy became easier. When I started viewing my husband as a gift to be thankful for, I began seeing him differently. He became desirable and handsome again. I was happy to see him each day. His touch became pleasing again and the warmth of his body warmed my heart.

With prayer and thanksgiving, the improvements in our marriage were immeasurable. They sparked a determination in both of us to continually search for ways to make it better. We used marriage resources to continue our progress. We watched shows like *Marriage Today* and read books like *The Power of a Praying Wife,* by Stormie Omartian. We joined a couples group at church. We attended workshops and listened to podcasts in the car, seizing hold of every opportunity to keep positive marital vibes in the forefront of our lives.

Date nights became a must and we sent the kids to their grandparents for a week during the summers, simply to concentrate on us. We made intentional moves to improve our marriage and our marriage improved exponentially.

Today our marriage is happier than ever. We are committed to one another. I have his heart and he has mine. Instead of living each day, trying not to make each other angry, we seek out things, on purpose, to make each other happy. We communicate with one another and we slow-dance when our favorite songs come on, including the one from our canceled wedding. We respect one another. And, against all odds, we trust one another.

I know my story isn't your story, but your outcome may be just as good. It took a long time for us to get to this point, but I hope my experience can help you achieve a happy, healthy marriage, in your own time.

Forgiving someone who hurt you is hard, but you can do it! I've been where you are. I've stood where you stand. And I'm here to tell you to keep standing!

Here are tips that helped me through the many stages you'll encounter on this journey, from trauma to triumph. They were life-changing to me. I hope they will bless you too.

THE RAINBOW

GRIEF

NOW, WHEREVER YOU are in your journey, if you've been hurt and are still trying to manage it, you likely don't feel much like standing. In fact, you may feel more like lying down and never rising again. And like me, you will experience grief.

When you've endured heartbreak and the ending of a love relationship, grief will surely strike. And it is okay to grieve. Grieving never feels good, but it does let you know that you are still breathing, still living and still loving. It's a sign that there is still life in you and where there's still life, there's hope.

There are many stages of grief and you may endure them all, or just some. But know that they are natural and to be expected when experiencing a great loss.

One of the first stages you will encounter is a state of shock.

Not only will you experience the initial shock from the discovery that your partner has cheated, but you may be in a traumatic state of shock that will take some time to recover from. You may experience the type of shock that comes from being in a terrible accident or witnessing a horrific event. You will feel like the victim of a tragedy and it will take some time to shake that off.

It may come with a numbness of mind and emotions and a crippling of your spirit. You may feel as if nothing matters and sit and stare at the wall for hours on end, wondering how you ended up in this place. You'll be searching for answers that make sense and finding no solutions. And you will find little comfort in the words of others.

You'll feel like you have no worth, because no one who's treasured would be dealt the kind of hurt you're experiencing. Drowning in your feelings will be your number one priority and self-care may become nonexistent.

You will also likely experience denial, a stage where you know this has really happened but refuse to accept it. You will cry your eyes out and sit around waiting for the phone to ring or a text to ping, only to find that it won't, and yes, your phone IS still working. You'll go to bed at night fully expecting that when you rise the next day, all of this will have just been a bad dream. You may even go about your normal daily activities, expecting him to be home for dinner, like always.

Denial postpones accepting the reality you eventually must face. It eases your pain for a while like a good narcotic. But, it also puts off the parts of the grieving process that you need to go through to get to a place of acceptance, wholeness and forgiveness.

If your spouse has cheated, you will want to know every sordid detail about the affair. It will be your mission to know every who, what, where, when, why, how and every how often (which you'll know is different from every how). You'll believe that knowing everything there is to know about his misdeeds will somehow make you better off, as if the knowledge will numb the pain.

But it won't.

Knowing that they met every Tuesday at 2 p.m. at the Gladstone Motel on Fifth Avenue, or that they met at your son's soccer game while you were having gallbladder surgery, will not make you feel better. Knowing that she's a large-breasted redhead named Adriana will not ease your pain. And finding out she's an accomplished lawyer with a booming practice that was just featured on the news, will not help you sleep at night.

I'm not saying don't ask him, and I'm sure you will. I am telling you from experience that it's not likely to make you feel better.

It's not going to help if you set the Gladstone Motel on fire or make your son quit soccer. And your spouse won't be hurt if you never wear red again or drive to his lover's office to write "Adriana is a whore," on the hood of her car. But you're sure to have these thoughts, at times.

Rest assured, others who've stood where you stand, have had them too. Because your desperate need to know everything is part of the process of grieving a breakup. And you'll think you want to know it all until you discover that you really didn't want to know it ALL.

And whether or not you know it all, you will likely go through a period of anger. You will be angry with your partner and possibly angry with yourself. And maybe even angry with God.

You will resent your partner for not cherishing the love and trust you had in him and, if married, your wedding vows. And, if the affair involved your home or your car, you will feel as though he took what was pure and tarnished it, what was clean and made it dirty. You will feel as though he was driving the truck that ran you over.

And there may be periods where you fall into self-loathing. You will look at yourself and think, "I knew he was a breast man. Why didn't I get a boob job?" or, "Why couldn't I just lose weight after the baby?"

You may blame yourself for not seeing that he was unhappy or not paying closer attention to your bank statement. You might magnify your imperfections and wonder how you could have been so blind. You may vilify yourself and make him the victim.

And you will find that your anger extends well beyond the two of you. You will very likely be angry with his lover. Whether you know her or not, she will become public enemy number one. To you, she will be the slut that broke up your marriage. She will be the HER in your book. You will wonder why she didn't have the morals to just go for someone who was available. She will be branded a homewrecker. You will become her judge, jury and execution-er, and you will consider her the scum of the earth.

Unless, of course, you discover she had no idea he was married and wants nothing else to do with him, in which case, you may show her some leniency. If this happens, you still won't like her but you may not hate her as much. And eventually, you may see that she too was a victim.

Your anger may take on other targets, as well, such as your husband's friends and relatives, or anyone who knew and didn't tell you. And it will extend to anyone who sympathizes with him, in any way.

If your mother tells you that you should give him a second chance, and you're not ready, she'll take her place on the list. If your pastor advises you to forgive him, and you're not ready, he too will take a number. No one will be exempt from a possible spot on your list and there's no telling how long they'll remain there, because you're grieving and grief knows no timetable.

And then, there's depression. Depression will almost always accompany grief. Depression will cause changes in your attitude, your outlook on life, sleeping and eating habits, relationships, and the list goes on and on. Depression will make your future appear grim. You will feel lost and desperately sad. You will feel lonely, even in a crowd of supporters, and you may lose faith and hope.

And when your faith is in turmoil, your

anger may turn toward God. You will wonder how God, in all of His goodness, could allow something so awful to happen to you. You will wonder why He doesn't wake you up from this nightmare. You'll ask Him why, if He so loves marriage and so loves you, He would allow your marriage to fail.

You'll think you're getting back at God by not attending church or ceasing to read the Bible. You'll forget for a while that God's love for you doesn't depend on whether or not you like Him at the moment. You'll run from Him, instead of reaching out to Him for His help. And you'll think that you can barter with Him, like He's on your level. You'll promise Him that you'll start going to church or stop cursing if He just brings your husband back. As if there's some power you have that He doesn't, or something you can offer Him that He doesn't already have.

And if your anger and depression go unresolved, they will turn into a bitterness that will steer the trajectory of your future relationships with Him, your family and your spouse. And if you stay in that state, it will inevitably affect your children.

So grieve…you will. Seek help…you should. But overcome…you must!

And overcome…you can!

Jeremiah 1:19 says, "They will fight against you but will not overcome you, for I am with you and will rescue you, declares the Lord."

You do have the power you'll need to get through this. And though it may seem impossible, tissue-free days are on the way.

The phase of grieving that will bring you to a place where you can think rationally and make future plans is acceptance. In the acceptance phase, you will finally come to grips with what has happened. Denial will take a back seat to reality, and though you may still be angry, you will be able to temper it enough to go about the business of establishing your new normal. You will be able to think forward, engage in conversations that are reasonable and make decisions that are sound.

There's no universal stopwatch for grieving. You will grieve as long as you need to, and the phases can come in any order, at any time. With acceptance, there may still be anger and possibly depression. There is no road map to it.

Though others have traveled this road before you, no one has walked your exact path. Your situation is unique, your pain is your own and your journey to wellness is uniquely yours. Don't judge your progress based on anyone else's.

Your situation may involve a longtime boyfriend and not a spouse. Or the one who betrayed you might be your first and only love. Or this could be the third husband who has cheated on you. Whatever the situation, you are entitled to your feelings and entitled to your time to grieve and to heal.

If you are in the process of grieving a lost love and feel you cannot go on, please seek help. Let someone know how desperate you are feeling. You will find that there are plenty of others who have stood in your shoes and lived long, happy lives to tell about it. You have nothing to be ashamed of. We all need help sometimes. So tell a counselor, a trusted friend, a pastor, a teacher, a support group or someone on a hotline that you need help.

When you think you don't have the strength to get through the agony of betrayal, know that God can show you strength you didn't know you had. And when all seems so hopeless that you don't even know what to pray, the Holy Spirit will give you the words you need.

Romans 8:24-26 says: "For in this hope we were saved. But hope that is seen is not hope at all. Who hopes for what they already have? But if we hope for what we do not yet have, we wait for it patiently. Likewise, the Spirit helps us in our weakness. We do not know what we ought to pray for, but the Spirit himself intercedes for us through wordless groans."

Talk to God about your despair and pray for Him to help you see your way through. Ask God to comfort your heart, ease your troubled mind and bring you to a place of peace. Once there, He will guide your steps and provide you with the insight you'll need to determine if your marriage is worth saving.

Even if you've already decided that your husband will not be a part of your future, ask God to direct your path so that you, as an individual, will be able to overcome this experience and go on to foster healthy future relationships.

The time will come for you to stop grieving and when it arrives, you'll know. So, keep kicking and rising upward. You'll eventually reach the surface, breathe and feel the sunlight on your face again. And if all you have left in you is a doggy-paddle, do what you can and trust God to do the rest.

Isaiah 40:31 says: "But those who wait on the Lord will renew their strength. They will mount up with wings like eagles. They will run, and not be weary. They will walk, and not faint."

So faint not, my friend. You will not fall. God's got you!

HE SAID, SHE SAID

IF YOU'RE THINKING about rebuilding your broken marriage, there are several things you must remember.

One of the most important is to **stop talking badly about your spouse.**

Now, I know this is easier said than done. I know you've been wounded. You've experienced unfair, unsolicited, life-altering pain that was hand-delivered by the one you loved the most.

What he did was a terrible thing. He caused you trauma, stress, strife and nearly made you lose your mind, and possibly your life.

He didn't take time to think about how his behavior would affect you, or worse, your children. He didn't ask you if this was a good time to ruin your life and your love. He didn't consider any consequences.

He didn't think about how you were supposed to be able to pick yourself up, go to work each day and interact with others as if nothing had happened. He behaved like a brut, a stranger, a person who has no morals or values, a person unworthy of trust.

But guess what?

Deep down inside, you still love him. He may genuinely want your forgiveness and the pain in your eyes, alone, likely makes him feel just as bad as you hope it does.

Don't make the mistake of thinking that calling him every bad name you can think of and telling your family and friends how awful he is, will make him somehow feel the exact depth of the pain you feel.

As much as you want him to, he can't actually relate to what you're going through.

Sure, he can see the tears in your eyes and he can tell that you are hurting, but he doesn't feel what you feel and he doesn't truly comprehend your devastation. Though his heart may be heavy for the pain he's caused, it's not broken.

You wish he could help you carry this pain. And that makes sense. Because as husband and wife, you're supposed to bear one another's burdens and sorrows. He made a commitment to help you through life's troubles, for better or for worse, and nothing could be worse than what you're feeling.

So you find it very difficult to navigate this

tough season without his support and, if he's your best friend, you feel as though you've lost that too. And you'll want the world to know that he's a jerk.

But the fact that he doesn't seem as depressed as you are or look as broken as you do, does not mean he doesn't care. The fact that he's not drowning his sorrows in a tub of cookies and cream, does not mean he doesn't regret what he's done. And his not calling you five times a day to check in, does not mean he's forgotten your pain. In fact, the hurt in your eyes and the pain in your voice, may actually be more than he can face.

As much as you want him to feel, appear and be as upset as you are…it's just not going to happen.

Oh, how I wish someone had told me, during the years I talked badly about and to M, that my behavior was not endearing him to me, but prolonging our disconnection from one another.

Sure, it sounds obvious, but when you're the receiver of a terrible wrong, the instinct to inflict pain comes naturally and often. I wish someone had told me that although he was the villain, a man will only take so much aggression and finger-pointing before he reaches a point where his regret for the pain he's caused becomes regret for sticking around to put up with your verbal abuse. And no matter how remorseful he may feel, if you put him in a position where he feels like there's nothing he can do to make things right, he'll eventually stop trying, because it's pointless to invest in a useless endeavor.

And some men, if accused enough times, will say, "Well, since she's so sure I'm still cheating, I may as well cheat," because they'll feel they should do something to deserve the mistreatment they're getting.

Now it will be hard to talk nicely for a while, because of the immense pain he's brought you. And hurting people hurt people. But if you've mutually determined that you want to stick things out, you're going to have to put in the effort to be mindful of what you say.

Tarnishing his reputation will not improve yours and it may even chase people away. Your loved ones realize you're hurting, and they know who caused it. And he's quite aware of it, too. There's no need to constantly remind the world.

And, by all means, do not launch a verbal assault on the things that make a man feel like a man, for this is one area of attack from which he may never rebound, or at least not for you. And if you hope to reconcile, you'll want his particulars to participate and his junction to function.

If you want to keep him, you must resist the urges that will surely come, to remind him of his wrongdoings.

Every word you speak against him is planting the seed of a poisonous fruit. And it's taking root in your soul and that of your family. It's being heard by your children. It is affecting the way your friends and relatives feel about him and, if you decide to forgive him one day, it doesn't mean *they* will.

So, if there's any chance at all that you will consider reconciliation, throw that poisonous fruit on the ground and watch it splat like the rotten tomato it is. Use your words to plant seeds of hope and watch them blossom into stems of strength, leaves of love and petals of perseverance.

The power of life and death is in the tongue (Proverbs 18:21). Speak life to your relationship. Tell the little devil that's whispering in your ear to pitch its fork elsewhere. Let your mouth be fertile ground where your words sow strength, growth and renewal.

I know it's hard not to bad-talk him. I did it and it cost me years of discontentment. But until you get to a place where you can say something positive, do like your mama once told you and don't say anything at all. Because you never have to take back an unspoken word.

TIT FOR TAT

O NE EASY AND very likely thing to do when you're dealing with the hurt of a lover's betrayal is to find yourself a lover.

And why not, right? After all, you're justified, aren't you?

Won't it make you feel better to know that someone else finds you attractive enough to sleep with? And, if your spouse discovers it, he can't possibly get mad after what he's done. Right?

Wrong.

If you are truly sincere about repairing your relationship with your spouse, you must resist the temptation to go tit for tat. Quite literally, in fact.

You must again follow Mama's sage advice, "Two wrongs don't make a right, Baby."

Bringing other people into your life while you're overflowing with emotion will do nothing but muddy the waters. Your mind will be confused, your vision will be blurred and it's hard to make forward steps when you're sloshing through the debris and contamination that an extra body will bring. You won't be able to clearly see the things that are necessary to reach your goal of reconciliation. You'll be blinded by the temporary euphoria of feeling like you've gotten even with your spouse or the momentary misconception that the person you're sleeping with isn't taking advantage of your fragile emotional state.

You will miss the progress your spouse is making. You will overlook the gestures, however slight, that your partner has done to show you they really do love you. And, you'll be in the middle of a mess of your own creating. You'll be using that other person. You'll be the jerk. You'll be the one responsible for purposely causing another's pain.

If reuniting with your spouse is really your goal, you must stay focused on that singular objective.

Sure, you could go out and have a one-night stand, but to what end?

A one-night stand to you might be a serious event for your one-night partner, whose mental and emotional state you have no control over and no prior knowledge of. And wouldn't it be just your luck to end up with a psycho?

And you won't feel better, not permanently at least.

You'll have fleeting moments of pleasure that will last as long as your tryst does, and then they'll disappear, because your true self longs for real love and your heart will know that your fling is not the real thing.

Your heart will yearn for that "skipping through the grocery store together" love, that "wrapping your arms around my waist and resting your head on my shoulder" kind of love. That "it's okay if you go to the bathroom while I'm in the shower" kind of love. And your heart will know the difference.

In the game of tit for tat, you'll likely end up with a place mat...a single-purpose, disposable partner, put in place to collect the crumbs of your broken relationship and to soak up the spills of your tears. And place mats end up in the trash.

So don't waste your time trying to one-up your spouse. Invest your time in getting yourself together and evaluating if your relationship is worth saving. Life is too short to play around. And, in the game of revenge, nobody wins.

Seek the Right Counsel

S O YOU'VE GOT all of this stuff you need to talk about and all of these feelings and emotions you don't know how to deal with. And what do you do when the person you tell your innermost thoughts to is the person you no longer trust? Who do you turn to?

Your natural instinct will be to turn to your friends and family. You'll seek out those who have loved you from the start and in whose confidence you can trust. Those who will soothe your wounds. And getting the support of those who know and love you is crucial. But you must be selective about which friends and relatives you choose, not because they're untrustworthy, but because you're likely to call up Cousin Pookie and the Posse, who will devise a plan to make your spouse pay for the pain he's caused you, in ways that might not be legal.

By all means, lean on your loved ones, but choose the upright ones, not the uptight ones. Psalms 1:1-2 says: "Blessed is the one who does not walk in step with the wicked or stand in the way that sinners take or sit in the company of mockers, but whose delight is in the law of the Lord, and who meditates on his law day and night."

Seek out the advice of those who you know won't lead you to key his car or put sugar in his gas tank. And, if that's your mother, find another. If, like me, you've got a sister and nieces that will tear him to pieces, resist the urge to call them, because sometimes what sounds like a good plan in theory, cannot be stopped once the police arrive.

Seek out that friend who will not only pull you back from the ledge, but will tell you what you *need* to hear, not just what you *want* to hear.

And, if you don't have a friend like that, who else can you talk to?

There are many resources available for people who are looking for a support group. Libraries, churches and community centers host many support group meetings, and if you can't bear to leave home, join an online group. A simple web search for a group in your area might be just the thing for you. But do know that, if you're determined to make your marriage work, you may not benefit from a group of women or men who are simply sitting around bad-talking their spouse. And if this appears to be the group you've met, find one whose goal is the same as yours.

And if you can get your spouse to attend counseling, by all means DO.

I am not a marriage counselor, but I do suggest you try one. And if you try one, you've got to be tough. Attending counseling does not guarantee that your marriage will work and it doesn't mean that you'll come out feeling vindicated because you were the victim of a wrong. But it will provide you with an impartial person who has nothing to gain by telling you what the issues are in your marriage. And, when a spouse has strayed, there are often many underlying issues. Your problem is not simply that he cheated.

To this day, I do not know if our counselor, Jim, was trying some kind of reverse therapy when he suggested that "sometimes two very nice people just don't belong together," or if he was just giving his honest opinion. But, whatever the case, his suggestion prompted M and me to try to prove him wrong. And we did.

Jim also pointed out that M had a passive-aggressive personality, a trait that explained a lot of the triggers that led M to behave the way he did. And researching this personality trait has led me to understand how my behaviors could cause a passive-aggressive personality to kick into high gear, which is something I never would have known, without counseling.

I discovered, through researching this personality type, how my insistence that M propose to me by a particular date was a catalyst for M engaging in behaviors that were justified, in his mind, for insulting him in such a manner. They were a secret payback for pressuring him into doing what may have come naturally, otherwise. I learned that a passive-aggressive personality, though not outwardly aggressive, can be very angry or hurt inside but will often not admit it. Instead, they will engage in behaviors that silently, and seemingly unintentionally, impede your progress and their own.

I also learned to never give ultimatums. If you're dating someone and you think he should have proposed by now, you likely have valid reasons for believing so. But, take my word, nothing good can come from giving him an ultimatum.

Ultimatums are a combination of unwanted pressure and a threat. They cause resentment, anxiety and fear, none of which are good or godly. So be very careful when playing the ultimatum game and, better yet, avoid it altogether. Making someone feel like they have no choice is no way to go into a marriage.

Ultimatums may work with children, but your mate is not a child. And you are not his parent. No adult wants to feel like he's not in charge of his own decisions.

And if you are cohabitating, he likely feels even less of a rush to cement the deal. Because, in his mind, things will largely remain as they are. And, as a male, he doesn't have the same need to rush into a commitment because his biological clock is not on your timer.

This is not to say you shouldn't make your feelings known if you have been dating for a while and believe it's time to take the next step. It simply means that your discussion about your future should be a two-way communication, not a one-way command. Counseling helped me see that.

Our time with Jim was also critical in pointing out other faults. And they were faults of mine.

I went into counseling expecting to be heard, understood and justified. I was thrilled to have found a male counselor because I felt if a male told M how badly he'd behaved, he'd be more likely to accept his wrongdoings as universally wrong for any man.

My initial request was to be counseled by a person of faith because I thought if we could get a male counselor who was also a Christian, we'd have just what we needed. I wanted someone that would pummel M with scriptures about the sanctity of marriage and give him irrefutable evidence of how blessed he was to have me and how much he'd messed up. But, because Employee Assistance Program options can be limited, we ended up with ol' Jim.

But, in the end, it didn't matter that Jim never went to church. He asked me questions that really made me examine myself. Like when he asked me why, as a person of faith, I sat up and worried when M wasn't home.

And then followed with things like, "Shouldn't you have faith that God is taking care of him when he's not home?" (Psalms 55:22). And, "Doesn't the Bible contain scriptures about God not giving you a spirit of fear?" (2 Timothy 1:7). And, "Isn't there a scripture that says to be anxious for nothing?" (Philippians 4:6). And, "So, if you believe in these things, what are you sitting up worried for? Why don't you just pray for his safety and go to sleep?"

Jim questioned my faith so much that there were many times when I wanted to throw a projectile across the room and hit him in his forehead, but I feared he'd remind me that this too, was not very Christian. I didn't have a good answer for many of his questions and I was angry that he, who didn't even attend church, had been dabbling in my Bible. The nerve! He reminded me often that the faith I was professing was looking more like an act than an action.

But the most profound and life-changing thing Jim made me aware of was, by far, the fact that I was extremely bitter. When, after weeks of listening to my legitimate cries and concerns, he looked at me and said, "You are really bitter. If you've forgiven M, why are you so bitter?" he totally opened my eyes.

My friends and relatives had listened to my anger and animosity for years. They knew I was full of bitterness. Yet, they never said the words that would set me free. But Jim did. And a good counselor will do the same for you.

Jim helped me see that my constant criticisms of M hurt me as much as they hurt him and, if I didn't forgive and move on, I would be responsible for putting the final nail in the coffin of our relationship. And I'd have no one to blame but myself.

There's no shame in seeking assistance for your marriage. Counseling is hard, but it helps.

You won't always feel like it's worth it and it won't always feel good, but it's worth a try. It's not easy to critically see yourself through a stranger's eyes, but sometimes it's necessary to see yourself as others see you. So stand tall, go in with your ears and heart open, and find out some things about yourself you may never have otherwise known.

And don't think you'll whiz through it unscathed. There's a chance you'll fall off your holy roller skates and end up on your knees. But dust yourself off and try again. Seek out advice that's straight, no chaser. You're stronger than you think and you can take it. Let someone help you see what you've been missing.

FORGIVENESS IS FREE

UNTIL JIM POINTED it out, I was one big walking bottle of bitterness. I looked at M through bitter eyes, I spoke to him with a bitter tongue and nothing he did satisfied my bitter attitude.

If he brought home my favorite candy, I thought, "Now he KNOWS I need to lose weight. He must want me fat and ugly."

If he came home, handed me cash and said, "Here, honey, go out and buy yourself something nice," I thought, "Why doesn't he like the clothes I'm already wearing? Has he looked in the mirror lately? He should be buying himself something nice. And hitting the gym!"

And whenever he missed one of our kids' activities because of his work schedule, I'd make it seem like he missed out on their entire youth, to make him feel like a failure as a father.

There was truly nothing he could do that I wouldn't find fault with.

It's amazing he didn't give up and walk

away thinking, "What's the point?" Especially since he'd been asked to leave and had a chick on the side, ready to scoop him up at any time.

But through counseling I learned that my bitterness was directly tied to my unhappiness. I began to see that the person who chained me in a constant state of misery was me, and to free myself from the bitterness that bound my entire being, I had to forgive and move on.

For years, I held my forgiveness hostage. It was my collateral. It was my little way of saying, "I'm never, ever, ever going to let you forget that you did me wrong and nothing you can do will ever change that. You are forever in my debt!"

I spent years saving up my forgiveness for the magical day when he'd be perfect enough for me to grant it to him. A day that, as long as I was bitter, would never come. A day in which I'd release to him, after years of paying for it dearly, the very thing God has given us all for free.

In fact, if I had saved just a penny for each time I'd said something mean to him or thought something bad about him, I would have been rich, many times over.

I thought, since I'd stayed with M all those years, it meant I'd forgiven him. But it took a stranger like Jim, looking in from the outside, to tell me I was wrong. So, I decided to try forgiveness…the thing I thought I'd done, but really hadn't.

I thought about the words of Ephesians 4:32, which says, "Be kind and compassionate to one another, forgiving each other, just as in Christ God forgave you."

I thought back to all of the times I'd advised others to forgive someone for harming them, without realizing I was guilty of unforgiveness myself. I asked God to forgive me for withholding my forgiveness because I was wrong to associate such a great cost to something that should have been free. And now, years later, I can see that the greatest cost was not to M, but to me. For not only should I have freely given it, but by giving it, I became free (Matthew 6:14).

And this forgiveness thing became contagious. It spread through my life like a wildfire, burning the chains of bondage that had kept me from experiencing happiness in other areas of my life.

I came from a family that rarely showed affection. My mom was a good mother, but like her parents, seldom gave hugs and kisses or said "I love you." I always envied families who did, and I wondered why we couldn't be one of them. I went into adulthood carrying the same trait.

But, once forgiveness took hold of my life, I started ending calls with Mom with the words "I love you." And, after throwing it out there the first time, I said it every time she was about to hang up the phone. And she started saying it back. Now, years later, our calls always end with "I love you" from both sides of the phone and oftentimes, she even says it first.

Then this forgiveness train traveled to my father, a man who I grew up without, though we lived in the same small town.

My mom left my dad when I was just a toddler. I'm told their marriage was bad, and I don't know all the details, but one day while he was at work, Mom packed up my two older siblings and me, took what she could fit in the car, and never looked back.

What she couldn't grab, we never saw again, so I've never seen any of my baby pictures because they were left behind. This bother me when school would have those "Guess Whose Baby Picture This Is" contests, because all I had was a picture from when I was in first grade. People always knew which picture was mine, because I was the only one that had no photo to show that I existed before age 5.

My dad used to pick me up from my mom's and take me out on the weekends, until one day when I was about 9, he stopped suddenly, and without explanation. I used to sit back and try to recall what I did wrong that last time he dropped me off…what I did to make him no longer want me.

At the time, my mom was dating a man who had a young baby, from a former relationship, and the baby was visiting our house the day my dad last dropped me off from an overnight visit. When I entered the house, with my dad behind me, I saw the baby and jumped with excitement. The baby was cute and sweet and we'd never had a baby around the house before. I put down my bag and went over to hold the baby, and when I turned around, my dad was no longer at the door, waiting to kiss me goodbye. He was gone and he never returned to my mom's house again. And he didn't call. All I could think of was how awful I had been to not kiss him goodbye before running off to hold that baby. I wondered if he'd rejected me because he felt I'd rejected him.

For years I was tortured by the "why didn't my daddy love me" blues. I went from the extremes of feeling that I wasn't good enough for him to being angry with him. I felt that, even if he thought I'd rejected him that day, he, as the adult, should have gotten over that.

But the day I opened my heart to forgiveness, it became clear that it no longer mattered. I was in my 30s then and I decided to let my children grow up knowing their grandfather, and I have never been sorry I did. My kids are glad to have another grandparent, and when we visit him, he seems quite tickled by them. My father had 19 siblings and, through him, we now have a connection with the aunts, uncles and cousins we never knew, and that's a whole lot of love to have missed out on for more than 30 years.

One of the good things about forgiveness is that you don't have to actually go visit someone and say, "I forgive you," to give it. So, you don't even have, "It'll cost me bus fare," to use as a valid excuse.

Forgiving someone doesn't make you weak. In fact, it's just the opposite. It takes tremendous strength to forgive a wrongdoer.

Have you ever watched the news and witnessed a mother forgive a defendant that has taken the life of her child? There is a supernatural strength in that forgiveness, that few people have. But we all have enough to start with one small gesture.

A little forgiveness has the ability to impact entire generations. It can start by standing next to Aunt Mary at the family reunion and asking her about the weather back home or putting your arm around your sister in the Christmas photo. Aunt Mary will forgive you for breaking her favorite vase and your sister will forget you missed her birthday.

Sometimes, it just takes one gesture on your part that says, "Everything is going to be okay now," to start a chain reaction of forgiveness.

And did you know that many of the people you need to forgive don't even know that you're mad at them?

There are millions of people in the world who have offended someone, that don't even know it. And you are likely one of them.

They may know they wronged you at some point in your life, but they've moved on and forgotten all about the offense, and you. So why are you wasting an ounce of energy being upset with them? Why are you missing out on family reunions because Uncle Matthew is there? Why are you eating alone on Thanksgiving just because no one ate your dressing last year? Why are you not watching your kids grow up just because your ex-wife has remarried?

Do you know who is missing out because of

your pettiness? You are! You are the one who isn't sucking the ribs Aunt Sally brought to the reunion. You are the one who didn't get to hear Grandma's secret pound cake recipe and you are the one not giving away your daughter at her wedding. You are the one who is holding a grudge because your mother left her gold watch to your brother. And you are missing out on a whole lot of life because of it!

So, forgive them now and do it every day! Because to truly be set free, you can't forgive today and go back to being angry tomorrow. Forgiveness, like faith, is more than just a profession, it's an action. And, to experience its benefits, you must exercise it daily to ensure it is fully charged and operational. You'll be amazed by its energy, because forgiveness is a force that generates as much power as it gives.

So, take action with your forgiveness. Be bold with it! Open up the container of your heart and pour it out. Once it hits the light, it will spread. Pull out your forgiveness, hand it to the receiver and walk away like you dropped the mic. Make a list of the people you've been withholding it from. Call, visit or text them and make it not just your new-year but your *all*-year resolution. They won't be expecting it, but they may like it and you will feel better for it. And if someone you need to forgive is no longer alive, it is not too late. Forgive them in your heart and let it be well with your soul.

I'm not saying forgiveness is easy, but there are many, many sins in this world, and we're all guilty of some of them (Romans 3:23). But, in our self-righteousness, we think we should be able to assign a scale of worthiness, as it relates to forgiveness. We feel like certain injustices should carry more weight than others. We believe we have the right to convict and condemn based on our level of hurt and unhappiness. But Luke 6:37 says, "Do not judge, and you will not be judged. Do not condemn, and you will not be condemned. Forgive, and you will be forgiven."

What hope would we have if God hadn't forgiven us all? And what right do we have to withhold something of which God has given us an infinite supply?

Forgive those who know they've hurt you and forgive those who don't.

Because forgiveness is not for you. It is FOR you to GIVE.

Forgive Yourself

A s you're deciding if you can do this forgiveness thing or not, and you're taking inventory of the people who should be on your forgiveness list, it's important to remember that the person who's making the list deserves their fair share.

Yes, you made some mistakes. You were too busy with the kids to notice he was feeling neglected. The house was always a mess. You wore the same raggedy nightgown to bed each night with a head wrap that smelled like his socks.

You weren't enticing. You didn't kiss him hello or goodnight. You failed to support his dream of being a door-to-door fax-machine salesman. You forgot to pick up his tux the day of his awards ceremony. And the list goes on.

You had your chance to be the perfect little spouse and you threw it all away. You didn't get it right.

So you spend your days thinking about all of

the things you could have done, those you didn't do and those you could've done better. And you begin to believe he was justified in what he did because you weren't on your job. And you start to really hate yourself for it. And so, the search begins...

You begin to look for ways to punish yourself for your misdeeds. And you find them. You find them at fast food restaurants and the snack aisle where you shop. Or you see them at the liquor store and think, "This is just what I need." Or you find them in the arms of a stranger, because you don't deserve someone who really loves you.

Or perhaps you're the one who cheated.

You had a great marriage. Your husband wasn't home much, but he was working two jobs to take care of your family. He always let you drive the good car and you never once had to fill it up with gas. Your children adore him. You used to be jealous of how they ran to the door to greet him at night, but now you realize they just really missed him, because he worked so hard.

He was good to your family. Your mom always took his side in arguments. He bought you anything you wanted that he could afford and he was preparing to buy your dream home.

Then you blew it.

You fell for the advances of the car sales-man who promised you the ride of a lifetime. You met him for coffee. Then you met him for dinner. Then, unfortunately you met him for dessert.

And now your husband is devastated. He can't understand where he went wrong. He loves you and hates you at the same time, but he desperately wants to keep his family together. He's moved out for now, to figure things out and clear his head. And each day without him feels like death.

You caused him pain he didn't deserve and you feel like you've earned whatever comes your way.

So you engage in self-deprecating behavior, as days turn into months, because you're a disaster who can't get anything right. And there's no sense in trying to patch things up. Right?

Wrong!

Getting through the betrayal of infidelity is gut-wrenchingly hard work. It takes boldness, perseverance and mental, physical and spiritual strength. You can't just walk up to it and say

"BOO," and think that monster is going to run away and everything will be fine again. You have to work at it!

But how are you going to tackle this giant when your guard is down? How can you fight when you're entering the ring already defeated? How can you make it to the finish line when you've eaten so much you can barely walk? And how can you beat it when you're too busy beating yourself up?

During all the time you've spent being ashamed of the person in the mirror, what has changed?

What has improved during your period of disgust and self-loathing? How many of your mistakes disappeared? How much of the past has erased itself? How many scars have vanished? Did the hands of time turn back?

And how do you feel?

Are you healthy? Fit? What's your anxiety level? How's your energy?

The fact that you did something bad does not make you a bad person. It makes you someone who made a bad decision...which makes you human. And being human makes you a child of God.

And that relationship gives you 24/7 access

to communication with your Father, who wants to soothe the troubles of your heart. So, tell Him what you've done and how awful you feel. As it says in 1 John 1:9, "If we confess our sins, he is faithful and just and will forgive us our sins and purify us from all unrighteousness." So why would you forfeit such a great inheritance?

Why would you not grab hold of that life-line?

If you are wallowing in guilt and self-pity, that lifeline will come in handy, because, without one, you'll drown in it.

Think about what life would be like if we never forgave our children. If we constantly reminded them of every misdeed and never showed them grace. Every child we raised would grow up thinking they were damaged goods.

You are not damaged goods, you are a child of God. You are "fearfully and wonderfully made" (Psalm 139:14).

Nothing good can come of guilt and shame. And the longer you dwell in it, the longer it will take to get yourself to a place of healthiness. Whether you are the cheated or the cheater, you can't change what has happened. Not one moment of time you spend lamenting about what an idiot you were will change any of your past actions. Take the knowledge of how to do better and just do better.

Romans 8:1 says, "Therefore there is now no condemnation for those who are in Christ Jesus." So, stop condemning yourself. Be free.

Look in the mirror and say to yourself, "I forgive you. God forgave you. Let's move forward."

This may be something you have to repeat each day for a while, but eventually, like anything engrained in you, it will take root. And whether or not your spouse forgives you, your heart will be lighter, healthier and better for it, and your body may be too. So lighten your load and give yourself a break.

Christ died for your sins. Stop carrying around a burden that isn't yours to bear.

Hebrews 8:12 says, "For I will forgive their wickedness and will remember their sins no more."

"Their sins," doesn't just mean Sharon's sins or Michael's sins, but "their sins" means everyone's sins. And everyone includes you. So why are you weighing yourself down with guilt and shame when you could be walking in the light of forgiveness? Why carry the contents of your household on your back when you have the keys to a U-Haul?

Forgive yourself for losing your moral compass. We've all done something we regret and are not proud of. We've had moments that are not shining examples of what we hoped to be, or what we were intended to be. We all have sinned and fallen short of God's glory.

Forgive yourself for not being the best mom when you were at your lowest. If there's one thing I know about kids, it's that they are very forgiving. Don't be afraid to tell them you're sorry and promise them that things will get better. It's okay for them to know that you were down, but not out. They will see that, in life, they can be overcomers, just like you were. And your family will be stronger for it.

Forgive yourself for the time you spent worrying about what others would think of your situation. Accept that you took some foolish actions to impress others with your toughness and your resolve to avenge the hurt you felt. Acknowledge that you should've known better, then act like you know better. Follow your true heart.

Forgive your new reflection in the mirror. The person looking back at you is still you, but it's a much stronger version, because you've weathered a storm. You may be battle-torn and weary, lumpy and hungover, but you are here, you are alive, you are a survivor. Forgiving yourself will allow you to heal and "heal" is the first part of "health." Trade in your wounds for scars and your fears for faith and trust that God will help you get back into shape. Because even when you let yourself go, God never lets go of you.

Forgive yourself. You're worthy of it, you're entitled to it and you deserve it. Forgiveness is free for all of us. Dig in and take your portion.

Forgive Her Too?

So, you're probably wondering if I have forgiven HER.

After all, this is a book about forgiveness.

And to be brutally honest…I don't really know.

She was someone I knew, but she wasn't my friend. And I don't say that because she cheated with my man, because sometimes friends cheat with your man.

She was a lady that I knew my husband knew, who was friendly to me in the beauty salon. As she sat and listened to me and my stylist discuss wedding plans, she knew my fiancé was her lover. And she sat there and took it all in, like she was just an interested, friendly lady getting her hair done, excited about my upcoming nuptials. And that was, to me, a dual betrayal.

Now I'll admit, for a long time, I hated her. And I spent lots of time hoping she'd be the victim of an unfortunate accident or an incurable disease. But we never had a confrontation of any kind. There was no hair-pulling brawl and she never harassed me in a way that made me take off my earrings and put up my fists.

When I found out they were seeing each other again, I don't know if she allowed me to tell him my discovery because she felt she owed me, or what. But, at the time, I felt like that was the reason. And I'm sure she's the one who sent the "How to Tell if Your Man is Cheating" article to my house.

In a weird way, it was like she wanted me to know. Like she perhaps thought that my knowing about her would cause me to send him away forever, and he'd be hers at last.

Funny thing is, as big a role as she played in my misery, it was never really about her, to M.

When M and I broke up for that year, we both saw other people, but he rarely saw her. (I know this because I drove by her house on several occasions.) She was a refuge for his passive-aggressive behavior, and a place to escape to when he wasn't ready for a committed relationship with me, but she was never the holder of his heart.

After despising her for a while, I came to the realization that it takes two to tango. And no matter how much seduction took place, my man had his own mind, will and emotions. He knew right from wrong and he chose wrong. He may have been enticed, but he was not coerced.

And I want anyone who is bogged down with animosity towards that other woman or man to grab hold of the realization that a zipper works both ways. He can zip it up just as fast as she zips it down. He always has a choice.

Once I accepted that she couldn't have had him if he wasn't a willing participant, I acknowledged that there was nothing she could do to take him away from me, if he didn't want to be taken. There was no sense driving by her house to see if he was there, because I couldn't stop him from going, if that's where he wanted to be. Any amount of time they spent together, was time he willingly gave. And all my worrying about it wouldn't change a single thing.

So, I let it go.

I stopped driving by her house. And I stopped asking M when he spoke with her last (something I did every few weeks, just to make sure his answer didn't change). I stopped letting my anxiety over his next move take my attention, and began to focus my energy on what mattered most: getting myself together.

I have not laid eyes on her in years and could not tell you if she lives in my town, any longer. I don't stalk her on social media, haven't Googled her and could not tell you if she's dead or alive. I don't even know if they're friends on Facebook or LinkedIn.

Now when I say I don't know if I've forgiven her, it's because I've certainly never told her I forgave her and I haven't seen her to know what feelings would flow to the surface if I saw her. But, my heart feels like it has.

And I've prayed for her. I have prayed that God has given her the insight, self-esteem and wisdom to know that she's worthy of joy, faithfulness and a man to call her own...ALL her own. She's entitled to someone who won't take advantage of her loneliness, respects her completely and desires to be only with her. She deserves love and devotion, not a like and a share.

And I do know for sure that I let go of the power I had allowed her to have over my life, which is a huge part of the freedom that comes with forgiveness. And the lower case "her" in this chapter is no typo, because HURT minus HER equals her.

I'd like to think that just the passage of time would be enough to feel nothing if I saw her, but to be totally transparent, I'll tell you this: There's a woman I run into on occasion who cheated with my best friend's boyfriend, many years ago. My best friend and I despised her. And, to this day, I still roll my eyes when she passes by. And I have no good reason to do that, because she has never done anything to me. So, like everyone else, I'm a work in progress. You pray for me and I'll pray for you.

Don't give a place in your thoughts to people or things that don't deserve your time or your energy. Life is too short and your brain cells are too precious to waste on things you can't change and people you can't control.

The cost to hold onto stress is high. Letting it go is free of charge. So why sink when you can rise? Release the anchor of unforgiveness and watch your spirit soar.

HE'S GOT WORK TO DO

I F YOU'RE IN the early stages of reconciliation, you're in a place where you're hoping for a good outcome, but don't know what to expect. You want to trust him but don't know where to begin and you don't know if he'll commit to doing the things that are needed to rebuild your trust. But, guess what? It's okay to ask for them. He's got work to do.

If he is truly invested in rebuilding your marriage, he will honor any reasonable request to regain your trust. And reasonable depends on your individual situation.

It is reasonable to ask him to get rid of objects she gave him, and it is certainly reasonable to buy a new bed if an affair was had in yours. And your requests can extend beyond material things.

If he cheated on you with a girl from the gym or his office, it's reasonable to ask him to find another gym, or even another job. If he cheated on you with a neighbor, it's okay to request that you move to another neighborhood and, if he had an affair in your small town and everyone knows about it, he should consider your request to move to another town. If he had a one-nighter during a Friday night out with the fellas, it's certainly reasonable to ask him to curtail those activities. And if he had sex with the church secretary, then one of them should look for Amazing Grace in a different place.

The granting of these requests will be a good step toward rebuilding your trust. And these are wishes that he may quickly be able to honor. But don't make the mistake of thinking that your marriage doesn't matter if your request is simply outrageous. Don't ask him to choose between you and his kids. Don't ask him to move to another state, if he's the sole-caretaker of his elderly parents who can't relocate. Carefully and prayerfully consider your request.

For me, after multiple betrayals of my trust, there was only one thing M could do to make me believe he really wanted to work things out. I needed him to develop a relationship with God. And although he went to church with me previously, he had literally done just that…went *with* me. He had gone through the motions, enjoyed the music and the people, but didn't know God for himself.

And M, not being the humble type, was not someone who bowed down to anyone. He was very proud, intelligent and confident and considered himself quite the catch. At times he was quite conceited, in fact, and, knowing a little something about every subject, he felt he knew enough about God to get by.

I knew that with M, the only thing that would make me believe he could actually settle down and submit to marriage, the way God planned it, was for him to get to know the man with the master plan. And meeting the Master was the medicine that healed our marriage.

Though I couldn't initially see it, through eyes blinded by bitterness, M became someone new. He gained the knowledge that he was never alone, physically or in his thoughts, and this knowledge guides his actions and thought processes daily. And now that he has the knowledge of Christ, he's aware that he's responsible for his actions towards me. He knows that God honors marriage and he strives to follow God's specific guidance on how a husband should treat his wife. And most importantly, he knows the true meaning of love.

After the betrayals, my request for him to take a class at church was a reasonable one, not an ultimatum, with results that were more than I could've hoped for. And the same could very well work for you. If your spouse is a tough guy or a real manly man who will put up a fight, ask him to spend some time with the One who can knock some sense into him. Or, if he's just a real smarty-pants who thinks he knows it all, introduce him to the Omnipotent One who knew all the answers before there were questions. And if he's just a real jerk with a history of mistreating women, show him the One who can knock him on his knees and have him screaming Father, instead of uncle.

Ask him to go to church, but don't try to force him. Let God work in him whatever His plan is. Remember, changing him is not your job. And if he falls asleep in church, don't stress over it. All of the nudging, throat-clearing and brushing his arm with yours won't help keep him awake. He is hearing what God intends for him to hear, even through his snores. And if he doesn't like the church you're in, visit another. Every church wasn't made for everybody. Ask him to select one you both can enjoy. He will appreciate being involved in the decision-making and will more likely be alert during service at a place of his own choosing. And you will be thrilled that he took the time to make a thoughtful decision about it.

M did that for me and your spouse may do that for you.

If you ask him to go to church and he won't, it doesn't mean that God won't intervene in your marriage. It doesn't mean you can't go to church or pray for your marriage. And if you've never gone to church before, don't worry about it. Churches aren't places for people who've got it all together; churches are for people who *need* to get it together. And that's all of us. Churches are for broken people, so pick up your pieces and bring whatever you've got. And if you can't get to church, pray wherever you are, because wherever you are, God is there.

This is what worked for us and I'd suggest it to anyone. Whatever it is that your spouse can reasonably do to show they are serious about repairing your damaged marriage, you should ask. But think long and hard about it first. And be honest with yourself.

If you feel there is nothing he could ever possibly do that will make you trust him again, you may be right. You may never trust him again and you may never feel like putting in the effort to do so, and that is your right. You may have reached your "enough."

But should you consider reconciliation, remember that your requests must be reasonable. So, if you're in a fragile state, you may need to consult with someone stable and trustworthy to determine what reasonable is. Once you've done so, and make your requests known, his willingness to honor them will be a good compass for indicating your future direction.

SHOULD I TAKE HIM BACK?

I F YOU'RE THINKING that forgiveness means you have to give him another try...think again.

You do not have to go back to your spouse.

In fact, you do not have to enter into a relationship with anyone that you have forgiven for abusing or misusing you.

The fact that you've grown and blossomed into a person who recognizes the benefits of forgiveness does not mean that the person who wronged you has matured or changed, or come into the realization that you are something to be treasured. There are folks that will take your kindness for weakness and your forgiveness for granted. There are those that will assume that your forgiveness means they are entitled to a place in your life again. They'll take it as a sign that what they did was not that bad. And they are incorrect.

Not every person you know was meant to be in your life forever. There's great truth to the notion that everything has its season. And no one wants to be barefoot in a blizzard or wear a fur coat during summer in the Sahara. Anyone will freeze or overheat if exposed to the wrong environment for too long.

If you can't tell what season you're in because your spiritual thermometer's broken or needs a little adjustment, ask for help. Ask God to show you who is for you and who was meant to move on. And if you need help getting away, ask for that, too.

If you're not sure if you want your spouse back because you don't think you can ever trust him again, try trusting God first. Ask God to help you determine if your marriage is worth saving. And then trust Him to do so. And ask him for the courage to move forward in whichever direction he shows you, because either path will be full of challenges for you to navigate.

Only you can make the decision to work on your marriage, if that is your spouse's desire. And it is important that it is an actual desire, and not just willingness on his part. Let him make his case to you, if you want to hear it. It should not be necessary for you to chase him down.

Your spouse should clearly and definitively let you know that he wants *you* back. His behavior should leave no doubt. And, if you have asked him to live elsewhere for a while, he will choose where he resides, carefully. If he wants you back, he will not move in with his mistress.

If he tells you he can't just break things off with her, cold turkey, then you likely have a problem.

Or if he says he loves you both and he's not sure what to do, give him all the time he needs to figure it out. In fact...give him a lifetime to figure it out. But not YOUR lifetime.

And by all means, if he comes home one day and tells you that he is in love with another woman and he doesn't want to be married anymore...LET HIM GO!

A man who is that sure about leaving you has already taken plenty of time to think about it and has already made plans to make it happen. So, let him go! Don't fight him or try to convince him otherwise. His mind is already made up.

It won't seem right, it won't seem fair, and it won't even seem possible. But sadly, it happens sometimes.

But oftentimes, when a man cheats, he feels really bad about it. And when he is really contrite and says, "I never meant to hurt you," he means it. He may have acted without thinking of the consequences and would do anything for a chance to take away the pain he's caused you.

If you and your mate really want to reconcile, and are both willing to put in one hundred percent, you can do it. But be prepared that there may be some loved ones who will not support you. And you must be strong enough to tell those who are not in your camp to pitch their tent, and their opinions, elsewhere. It is up to you, not them, to decide the course of your marriage. And if they don't like it, then it may be that their season in your life is over. And if that should happen, forgive them too.

If you decide to let him go, you have a right to that decision. If you feel you can't move forward because he has fathered a child with another woman, no one has the right to make you feel guilty about not wanting to raise his lover's child. And no one has the right to mock you, should you choose otherwise.

Sometimes, the loss of respect that comes from the betrayal of an affair makes it impossible for a person to move forward with their spouse. As much as they might want to, they just aren't able to look at that person the same way again. The behavior they displayed throughout the course of the affair...the lying, the secret life, the deception...was so far out of character for their spouse, that they now see them as a stranger that they never really knew. And that's understandable, too. Ask God to help you discern whether it's worth working things out.

When contemplating whether or not to reunite with your spouse, it is important that you take a long, realistic look back at your relationship. Seek clarity because, during your separation, loneliness is sure to settle in, and when it does, the tendency to romanticize the former state of your relationship is highly likely.

It is very possible that the days, weeks or months spent apart will be filled with a longing for things to be the way they used to be, and your memory of how things used to be will be enhanced and possibly transformed into a relationship that never actually existed.

The good times you shared will become far more fantastic than they ever were, and the bad times will suddenly not seem so bad. Your desire to have him back in your life may blind you to problems of the past that may have played a role in the infidelity.

So it is very important, in your fragile state, to make an effort to be as realistic as possible.

And to do so may require the help of an accountability partner who knows your past relationship and loves you enough to be brutally honest with you.

You will need this person to remind you, when you're reminiscing about how perfect your honeymoon was, that your husband flirted with the concierge when he thought you weren't looking and wasn't in your hotel room one morning when you woke up.

You may need someone to help you snap out of it, when your eyes glaze over with happy thoughts of unhappy times and memories that never really happened the way you remember them now. Because loneliness will make your mind play tricks on you.

You will also need to beware of the biggest trap that awaits you during a period of loneliness and separation…a little thing called make-up sex.

Make-up sex is almost always pleasurable. By its very nature, it is intended to reseal a broken bond. It is designed to, at least temporarily, erase all pains and unpleasantries and replace them with feel-good endorphins.

And those endorphins will summon up feelings you thought you no longer had. They'll make you think that, if there's that much passion between you, then you must belong together. And in those moments, nothing else will matter.

But that moment of dramatic make up is usually followed by a period of traumatic wake up. You wake up to the reality that the thing that caused you to separate is still very real, and your relationship is still very broken. And there will still be much work to do.

And perhaps your stance on reconciliation is, "None of this would've ever happened if he was just more like me. I can change him. He can become the man I know he has the potential to be. He had a rough childhood, that's all, and he came from a dysfunctional family. He's broken, but I can fix that."

And you think, wonder, wish, want and hope that you can change him, because you know that all he needs is some tweaking and he'll be fine. He will never cheat again and you'll live happily ever after. Right?

Certainly!

There is an absolute possibility that he CAN change. There is absolute hope that a person can overcome all kinds of challenges. There is positively a chance that the problems of his past can be overcome and he can be all that you need him to be and more.

But YOU can't change him and it's not YOUR job!

Your job, should you decide to reconcile, is to love, honor and cherish him, for better or for worse. And doing that is critical because love covers a multitude of sins (1 Peter 4:8).

Your job is not to judge him for thinking and acting in ways you wouldn't, because the fact is, he's not YOU. He's a masterpiece from God and, though he has strayed, he was wonderfully and marvelously made. The cracks in his design can only be fixed by the One who created him.

So, don't brush him off and brand him damaged goods because he's not like you. We all have blemishes beneath our surface.

With the help of the Master Designer, cracks can be repaired and holes can be filled. Ask God to instill the things in both of you that He knows are missing and to fix the things in both of you that are broken. Ask Him what your marriage needs to survive and, should you choose to stay, ask Him to give it to you. He will provide the cement, nails and supernatural sealant that you need to hold your marriage together.

Proverbs 3:5-6 says, "Trust in the Lord with all your heart and lean not on your own understanding. In all your ways submit to him and he will make your paths straight."

And if you've forgiven your spouse, but don't want him back, it's okay. There are no rules on how to survive infidelity, there are only suggestions. The point is to SURVIVE, and surviving has different definitions.

Sometimes surviving means living through it and moving on to live a happy, healthy life, alone or with someone else.

And sometimes it means living through it, moving on and eventually rebuilding a happy, healthy marriage. Ecclesiastes 3:1-8 says:

> "There is a time for everything, and a season for every activity under the heavens: a time to be born and a time to die, a time to plant and a time to uproot, a time to kill and a time to heal, a time to tear down and a time to build, a time to weep and a time to laugh, a time to mourn and a time to dance, a time to scatter stones and a time to gather them, a time to embrace and a time to refrain from embracing, a time to search and a time to give up, a time to keep and a time to throw away, a time to tear and a time to mend, a time to be silent and a time to speak, a time to love and a time to hate,

a time for war and a time for peace."

Pray that God will help you to clearly see what time it is.

The choice to rebuild is yours, and it's a hard one. And it's difficult to know who should only be with you for a season. Ask God to direct your path to a healthy, happy you. He'll be there to guide you. Thankfully He's not seasonal, but with you year-round.

NIPPY-HEADED

THERE'S A LITTLE thing in life I like to call Nippy-Headed. No, not nappy-headed, Nippy-Headed. Nippy-Headed people are those who live their lives being Needy, Insecure and Pathetic (N-I-P).

I started using the phrase after watching an episode of *Sex and the City* where Carrie was called out for being needy, insecure and pathetic in her devotion to Mr. Big. I was so impressed when Miranda called Carrie these words, that I promised myself to one day write a book about how to recognize when you're being a doormat. But to be truthful, I was too busy being Nippy-Headed myself, at the time.

For example: Remember all the miracle checks that never came? Well check this...

The reason I spent all that time praying for money that never arrived, was not just because I wasn't financially secure enough to make it on my own. I was also afraid that I could not survive without M and I did not want to live any less comfortably than I was accustomed to.

If that sounds familiar to anyone, I've been where you are.

Unfortunately, many women have been in this situation. Some have been careless with their money, hoping to one day find a Maserati to hitch their trailer to. And some earn just enough to get by. Now, I'm not judging you, because I've been both. I hoped to be attractive and smart enough to catch a decent guy. And I did. But when things went wrong, I didn't have the resources to escape to anywhere decent. I wasn't able to pack up and leave or just simply get away for a while to clear my head.

I also did not have the confidence to say to myself, "Just go for it. Leave! You can do this. It won't break you. You will come out better, you'll see!" I simply didn't think I could make it.

So, before Nana's word from the Lord, I stayed and endured because I lacked both the resources and self-esteem to leave. Thankfully, when I got my prayers right, God answered them. And my marriage today was totally worth the wait.

But I cannot overstress the importance of doing a self-esteem check on your life. Make sure you're someone who doesn't have to put up with a bad situation, because you, personally, don't think you're able to stand on your own. Be someone who's confident you can make it, so any man who approaches you, dates you or marries you will know that you are not someone to be taken advantage of. Don't be insecure, needy or pathetic. Don't be that woman who's being dragged down the street, holding onto the bumper of his car. If he walks away from you and doesn't come back, then it wasn't meant to be. So, get up!

Do you know how important self-esteem is? Self-esteem is EVERYTHING! Without it, we are powerless.

A deficit of self-esteem causes us to relinquish the wisdom to turn around when we see caution tape straight ahead.

It compels us to bypass the brakes when a crash is approaching that will cause catastrophic damage to our lives.

It turns a blind eye to that skidding 18-wheeler that is about to total our vessel, rendering us emotionally and spiritually paralyzed, crushed and expelled to the ground.

It keeps us in a submissive posture, willing to put up with almost anything, sacrificing what's best for us for the ability to have someone to wake up with or help pay our bills.

We overlook how they're treating us, beating us and leading us astray, and we stick around, trampled and defeated, waiting for our next disappointment.

Ladies and gentlemen, get up and get your self-esteem back! Or, if you've never had it, there's no better time than now to invest in some. And just like forgiveness, self-esteem is free!

When you sit back and think about it, isn't it funny how many situations you've gone through, put yourself in and regretted that could have been avoided if you'd just had a healthy dose of self-esteem?

Or if you'd just thought you were worth so much that anyone would be foolish to lose you?

Or if you felt that you were good enough, smart enough or pretty enough?

If you believed that you were a prize?

If you felt it was a privilege to be in your presence?

If you knew there was nothing wrong with being alone and you were comfortable with the fact that you could make it on your own?

If you recognized that you are not responsible for fixing all that's broken in someone else's life and that failure to do so is not *your* failure?

If you believed that you deserved the best?

If you knew that you were good enough, just the way you are, and don't need anyone to mold you into their idea of how you should be?

What catastrophic relationships could you have avoided if you had just believed these things? Would you have looked for a better job or a nicer neighborhood? Would you have dared to apply for that line of credit, or perhaps a mortgage? Would you have gone back to school?

One's capacity to be insecure, needy and pathetic lies in the extent to which they lack self-esteem.

Have you done a self-esteem check lately? Ask yourself these questions:

Before you found out he was cheating, did you accept his lies, knowing they were likely untrue?

Did he spend time dishonoring your faith or your ability to freely worship?

Did he make your children part of his escapades and swear them to silence?

Was he verbally or physically abusive to you or your children?

Were you the primary breadwinner while he spent money on his mistress?

Were you catfished into marrying him?

Are you afraid you'll lose the chance to

reunite if you don't sleep with him?

Is he using the kids to guilt-trip you into reconciliation?

Are you allowing him to continue to see his mistress?

Was he your long-time boyfriend who says that, because you weren't married, he technically didn't cheat?

Are you trying to do things to improve your life, like finish school or start working again, but he's pressuring you to stop or causing a distraction?

Has he threatened to harm you or himself if you don't reconcile?

Does he say you'll never find anyone as good as he is?

Does he body-shame you into thinking no one will want you?

If you answered "yes" to any of these questions, there's a good chance that you are Nippy-Headed.

But fear not! Nippy-Headedness is correctable. It's just not where you want to stay.

You want to be that person who knows who she is and whose she is! You are a child of God! And as such, you are an inheritor of the promises of God, and His promises for you are great! So, there's no need to settle for less. God promises you can do ALL things through Him (Philippians 4:13). So, you don't have to stay needy, insecure or pathetic. You already have all you need.

You don't have to accept lies. You deserve to be told the truth.

You are more than good enough. You were made in God's image (Genesis 1:27).

You are above and not beneath. You are not his doormat (Deuteronomy 28:13).

There's no condemnation in Christ. Do not fall for his guilt-trips (Romans 8:1).

And above all else, it is never acceptable for you or your children to suffer abuse. So, if that has happened now or in the past, you must seek help!

It's okay if you're confused about what to do next with your relationship…whether to take him back or not…but if he abuses you or does not respect you, he is not for you.

Don't forget to turn to God when you don't know what to do. Seek out the One who is available for you to talk to day and night. He holds all of your answers and knows exactly what you need to get through any situation.

See yourself as God sees you and you'll know you are a force to be reckoned with. Not just in your current situation, but for the rest of your life. A healthy sense of self-worth will help you prevent toxic relationships, walk away from bad ones and get over them once you get out.

Work on building your self-esteem and, if you don't know how, ask God. If you don't believe in God, ask a parent, a mother, your auntie, a good friend, a counselor, a minister or someone you can trust, to help you in the areas you're struggling with.

If you put up with mistreatment because you fear loneliness, surround yourself with a good group of friends, or just one good one. And for company on those lonely nights, consider rescuing a pet. But have human friends too, because more than three cats + no friends = Crazy Cat Lady.

Truth be told, if my self-esteem had been higher during M's cheating days, we likely wouldn't be where we are today. I probably would've left him, confident I'd survive and I likely would've been fine. But in the words of the great Maya Angelou, I "wouldn't take nothing for my journey now." I lived and I learned and I'm now better for it. I am a witness of how gaining self-esteem leads to gaining the respect of others. And those who respect you, value your worth.

So, forgive yourself! We are all works in

progress. Don't beat yourself up about being Nippy-Headed for a season. It was a learning experience and now you know better. There is no perfect human so don't try to be a perfect one, just be a self-confident one!

Self-esteem is the perfect shampoo for a bad case of Nippy-Head. So, lather it up, rinse out the gunk and restore your beautiful shine. Then walk around confident that you can make it with or without him. And you will!

Let's Talk About Sex

Forgiveness isn't the only thing I withheld from my husband as punishment. I also withheld sex. And not just the act of intercourse, but intimacy, passion, cuddling…all of it.

Initially, the lack of sex was not intentional. It was more about the lack of love I felt toward someone who had caused me so much pain. It was about not wanting to be touched by hands that had caressed another, not feeling excited by the hands of a heartbreaker.

And those feelings continued for a long time.

When he tried to touch me, I wondered if he'd touched her that way. And sometimes, because I knew her, I'd picture them together, rolling around in bed, laughing at me. And I wondered if he used a condom with her at all.

I asked him about it twice. At first I asked him if he'd used a condom with her and he said "Yes." But, I didn't believe him. I didn't believe that in their moments of forbidden pleasure, he took the time out to say, "Hold up. Let me get a condom."

I didn't believe him because that's just not how it happens in the movies and when I pictured them together, I imagined all of the breathless longing and desire you see on film.

His answer upset me even more because it made me wonder why he was even carrying condoms. If he didn't leave the house expecting to have sex, how did he just happen to have a rubber ready?

Though he said he'd always worn a condom with her, his answer haunted me for a long time. It bothered me because I knew he was lying and I was worried about what his unprotected sex meant to me. I knew that a big disease with a little name was being passed around and was not something I cared to get. I worked with a man who was dying from it at the time and I did not care to become its next victim.

So, one day, I asked him again. I told him to look me straight in the eye and tell me if I had any reason to go get an AIDS test and he said "No." I told him I deserved to know if he had sex with her without protection, at any time, and he said "No." I told him that we didn't know the history of her partners and that my very LIFE depended on his answer. And he looked down, sighed and finally told the truth.

The truth was that he hadn't always used protection and didn't want me to know, but he couldn't live with the knowledge that my future well-being, with or without him, lied in his hands.

Now there's no bigger passion-killer than thinking about how your partner could not only break your heart, but endanger your future. And getting over this was no easy task.

So, for quite some time, my thoughts about him and sex were consumed with dealing with this knowledge. And, although it hurt deeply, I appreciated the fact that he finally came clean. I eventually stopped thinking about it daily, but it took several months.

For the years we were working things out, our sex life was nearly nonexistent. He would initiate sex and sometimes I would accommodate him, but it was simply that…an accommodation. I was a room with a vacancy and he was a messy overnight guest. I never initiated it and, while allowing it, never did much to participate. My bitterness played a large part in this because I was always mad at him and, as I asked him in those days, "Why would I want to make love to someone who is always doing something to make me mad?" So, I rejected his advances as often as I could and accommodated the rest like a good host. Though, looking back now, I realize that there's nothing he could've done that I would've been pleased with.

But, rejecting your spouse affects him in more ways than one. The resulting effect can be depression, anger and resentment, all of which will have an impact on you.

Rejection affects his innate desire to supply both your needs and his, and when a man feels unneeded and unwanted, you're walking in dangerous territory.

The anguish of nonperformance is not only mental, but can have a long-lasting physical impact. Our body parts need exercise and we all know what happens to muscles that aren't exercised.

Time is one thing you will never get back and your body is the youngest it will ever be, right now. So, if you're waiting years to forgive and move on with freely loving your mate, be advised that his lack of exercise, combined with age, may bring a new challenge for you to solve. And I hear the prescription is quite expensive.

Withholding sex from your spouse is never a good idea. You were meant to procreate and to find pleasure in one another. Sex is important to any marriage and especially important to men, not because they're horny freaks, but because God made them that way. So, if you're hoping to mend your broken relationship, know that you will eventually need to put a real emphasis on making things right in the bedroom, which likely means giving him that "F" word... Forgiveness.

With true forgiveness, you're free to love and make love the way you want to and most importantly, the way God intended for you to. Forgiveness opens up parts of you that you didn't realize were closed and, bedroom-wise, I mean that quite literally. Forgiveness is the initiator of grace that allows you to be the initiator of pleasure. Forgiveness releases the pressure of built-up anger, allowing you and your spouse to release your built-up pressure (which you may have to muffle if the kids are home).

So, where's your forgiveness? I know you have it in you.

Isn't it time you give it up?

Forgive and Forget?

OFTEN WHEN WE think of forgiveness, we think of the term, "forgive and forget." But does forgiving always mean forgetting? Can you have a successful marriage if you forgive without forgetting?

Yes, you can.

Infidelity is a traumatic experience and like all traumatic experiences, it is something you'll never forget.

You'll want it to disappear, to be untrue, to be just a bad nightmare that you will wake up from, but the fact is, it happened. And as the old saying goes, "Sometimes bad things happen to good people."

But the fact that you won't forget it does not mean that you should forever hold a grudge against those who hurt you or set about making their lives miserable. It doesn't mean you should think about it daily and make them pay for the rest of their life. It also shouldn't mean that you remind your spouse of their past deeds each time you have a disagreement. So, don't challenge Meryl Streep for the best actress Oscar by looking destroyed and despondent all day. Stop smearing your mascara when you know you'll be seeing him. He knows you. He's aware you've spent a lot of time in tears. You can only pound your fists on his chest and scream "Why," so many times, before it becomes overdone.

What happened is in the past, and replaying it in your head will only make you miserable and stall any real progress in your pursuit of a happy marriage. Instead of worrying about how you will ever forget what has occurred, you should focus your thoughts on filling your life with ongoing future good memories. You should forget about forgetting it and focus on forgiving it, because not one moment spent stewing about the past will change one moment of what happened.

You have control over your thoughts. Take sovereignty over your mind. You have the ability to focus on whatever keeps you healthy and makes you grow. You can make the healthy choice to leave a valley of chronic depression and hurt. Instead of focusing on what harmed you in the past, you can set your mind on what will lead you to a brighter future. You can choose to focus on moving forward.

Romans 12:2 says: "Do not conform to the pattern of this world but be transformed by the renewing of your mind. Then you will be able to test and approve what God's will is-his good, pleasing and perfect will."

Every experience in life, even those that hurt us, happens for a reason. And there is a lesson to be learned in each of them. The resulting outcome of these experiences is largely dependent upon how we choose to weather these storms. Those who get wet, take shelter, and come out clapping when the sun shines, do far better than those who get wet, angry, and carry an umbrella for the rest of their lives. And those who carry the umbrella of unforgiveness will always have a barrier between their lives and the warmth of the Son.

You will find that, when you practice forgiveness, the tragedy of this betrayal and others will fall further into the recesses of your mind, over time. As months and years of intentional focus on rebuilding your relationships pass, you will discover that the pain does fade. And, though it may not feel like it now, you will one day be able to talk about it like it's just another event in your life, if you choose to talk about it at all.

With the passing of time, you will not worry about where he's going when he leaves the house, and you'll look forward to seeing him when he returns. You will develop a heart for what makes each other happy and it will become your daily endeavor.

And when the past comes up, because you're watching a movie where it happens, helping a friend get through it or writing a book about it, the memories will remind you of just how far you've come. And the progress you've made will give you great joy and a tremendous feeling of accomplishment, because your relationship survived.

So, forget about forgetting and focus on forgiving because, as Jentezen Franklin says, "Forgiveness is not about keeping score. It's about losing count."

ALL CRIED OUT

ONE DAY, YOU'RE going to discover that you are all cried out. You will find yourself sitting around listening to the love song that always brings you to tears and you will see that you have no tears left to drop. Or perhaps one day, after a good long cry, you'll look at yourself in the bathroom mirror, mouth and chin covered in snot bubbles, with mascara streaks from eye to ear, and you'll say to yourself, "Oh my goodness! I'm a total mess." And you'll laugh hysterically.

When you get to that place, it's time to grab some tissues, take a shower, shave off your overgrown areas, do your hair and get on with your life.

It's time to invest in things that will improve your morale, your self-esteem and your health. And it's time to spruce yourself up.

When you're all cried out, it's time to start feeling better and looking better. And you may find yourself looking better than you did before!

It's time to try out that new haircut and color you always wanted to try. Or you may decide to add a couple of new pieces to your wardrobe. Because who doesn't like it when they're complimented on a new outfit or a new look?

The all-cried-out phase could be the time for you to start an exercise program or begin a healthy eating regimen to lose the weight you've always wanted to lose.

And what about that book club you wanted to join, or the class you thought about taking?

When you've reached the point where it takes actual effort to cry tears over your infidelity situation, it's really time to refocus that energy on yourself.

Engage in life again! Go for a makeover or a massage or, instead of sitting at home watching love stories, dress yourself up and go out to a movie or a play. Or sign up for a local volunteer opportunity.

You might even take karate lessons or join a line dance group. Or revitalize a skill you've allowed to lie dormant by picking up that paintbrush or camera. Or dust off your bike and your hiking boots.

Or, if you're a mom, now may be the time to get out and play with the kids again, or cook something more for dinner than a cup of mac and cheese. Living with a parent who is struggling with unforgiveness and long-term depression can have devastating mental, spiritual and developmental impacts on a child. Your children want and deserve a happy life and a happy you. Show them both are possible.

And, if you're a person of faith, build that up, too. Go to Sunday morning service, Monday night prayer, Wednesday night Bible study, Friday night revival and a Saturday night gospel concert, if need be. Read your Bible daily and pray for the wisdom to know your next steps.

And if you're not a person of faith, it's never too late to become one. Faith, like forgiveness, is free. And it's the ultimate exercise. You can take it up, have it, start it, practice it, step out on it, show it, keep it...and the list goes on.

Whatever you decide to do, now that you're better, get stronger!

Do it for the kids, do it for those who've been worried about you, but most importantly, do it for you.

Should you decide to give your spouse another chance, he will be amazed and in awe of the new remarkable you. But build yourself up so that you will be awesome, with or without him. Not just as good as before, but better.

And then what?

Working things out will be hard. But he may be worth the try.

He has apologized repeatedly. He has sent you flowers every day for six months. He has been living with his mother but still paying the bills at your home. Your best friend, who told you to leave him, has now changed her mind.

He's been going to church, stopped drinking and stopped bartending at the club where he met her.

He writes you old-fashioned love letters. And he still mows the lawn for your parents. He hired a plane to write "Please take me back," in the sky and you just found out from the nurse that he still visits your grandmother at the nursing home every Friday, because she thinks he's her son.

And he's asked for your forgiveness.

All of the evidence seems to indicate that this man seriously wants you back. And you do still love him.

So, what do you do?

You forgive him.

Because like all good things that God has given you an abundance of...love, talent and faith, to name a few, forgiveness comes in an unlimited supply.

In a life well lived we share our love, talent

and faith with others. And sharing them never leaves a void. Neither will forgiveness.

So, don't skimp and save and be miserly with it, because if you give it away, there will always be more.

It won't require a sale or a coupon, and it won't be marked down or on clearance.

In God's eyes, forgiveness is never discounted. For nothing that is priceless can be.

Starting from Scratch

Once you've gone down the road to forgiveness and decide your marriage is worth another chance, it's not a bad idea to start from scratch.

Erase the dust from the blackboard of your marriage and begin writing your story with a clean slate and a fresh piece of chalk. And do it before chalkboards are totally a thing of the past.

You could start from scratch by renewing your vows. Take the time to plan a nice wedding. Write new vows to one another. Seal your renewed commitment to each other with family and friends as your witnesses. Let the world see that you made it and have the celebration you deserve.

And, if your original ceremony was a shot-gun wedding, do it over again with no strings and no baby attached. This time you can do it by choice with far less hurry and worry.

And don't stop there!

Begin your new relationship like your old one began with some good old-fashioned flirting. Date your spouse like you just met. Call or text him to let him know you're thinking about him. Send him flowers. Wink at him. Hold hands when you're walking. Blow him kisses. Pat him on the butt when he passes you in the kitchen. Whisper sexy things in his ear. Wear something skimpy to bed or nothing at all. Go out on actual dates and when you pull back into the driveway, sit outside in the car and talk for a while before you go inside. Lay your head on his shoulder in the movies or at the park. And, if you have kids, kiss in front of them. It will both disgust them and make them feel secure at the same time, which is a win-win.

And don't forget the excitement that comes with making out in forbidden places. You can do that again too! Reinvent the quickie. Bring back the adrenaline that comes with the possibility of getting caught, but don't get arrested for indecent exposure and blame this book!

Another good post-infidelity benefit to starting your relationship anew is that you will now be privy to some things you may have previously done that were detrimental to your old relationship.

Through counseling or communication, you may have discovered that your spouse felt lonely because you were never home, or unwanted because you never wanted or initiated sex. Or maybe he was enticed by his lover because she complimented him, while you were always highlighting his faults or putting him down.

Whatever the case, in your renewed state, you will be armed with this knowledge and able to act upon it. You will be cognizant of these behaviors and the impact they had on your marriage, and you will take the necessary actions to prevent them from becoming problematic again.

In your new relationship, you may also find yourselves changing roles. You may have discovered through counseling that your wife was always tired because she worked full-time, came home and cooked dinner, washed dishes, cleaned the house, did the laundry and played chauffeur all evening. You may decide that you like cooking and could help with dinner a few nights each week. Or you could do a load of laundry, or take over one of the other household chores or carpooling duty.

Many women find that their spouse never looks sexier than when they are helping out around the house. And if your spouse has the primary responsibility for taking care of the children, your marriage could benefit if you schedule time to relieve them of their caretaker duties. Take the kids out for the day and bring them home tired and ready for bed. Give your spouse some sanity time and they will adore you for it.

And ladies, do your best to give your husband nag-free time. Let him enjoy his sports. Having a man cave does not mean he's deserted your cave. If he does the majority of the housework, lend him a hand. And the same goes for yardwork. If you look in the shed, you will find that the lawn mower is unisex.

Do what you can to alleviate stressors for one another and it will draw you closer. The best part is that you won't be doing it for the bedtime benefits; you'll do it because you appreciate each other and truly desire to make your marriage happy.

So, start over again with a fierce desire to make your marriage like new. Take new honeymoons. Say "I love you," each day. And be sure to keep your slate clear of any debris. No garbage from the past should go on it. And no one but the two of you should be allowed to write on your blank slate. Your board is for the new story that the two of you alone are writing, with no distractions or outside influences allowed. So, if you sense someone is trying to chime in on your masterpiece, snatch their chalk, throw it on the ground and stomp it to pieces! Because in the words my favorite quote from Kevin Ngo, "Until you run out of pages, there's still room to write an epic ending."

Pray Together to
Stay Together

MY HUSBAND AND I have been married now for almost 20 years, and I am thrilled to say that we are happily married.

Together we watched our daughter struggle through school with Executive Processing Disorder, a deficiency in organizational skills that are key to learning. Throughout elementary school, her reading and writing skills were far below grade level and she was painfully aware of that fact. One Christmas, when asked what she'd like Santa to bring, she replied, "I just want him to help me learn better, Mommy." And those words broke my heart.

We hired tutors, counselors and psychologists to figure out why she couldn't keep up. And when that didn't work, we tried meds, which, instead of swallowing, she hid between couch pillows and books. But around the time we started really working to repair our marriage, things changed. All of a sudden, things clicked for her and learning became easier. She began to comprehend things she had never understood before and the world opened up for her. Today I am beyond proud to say that she has graduated from high school with academic and athletic scholarships and has two parents that she often calls her "goals." And she is doing well in college.

She has no idea what it took to get us all where we are today and she has very little memory of Nana. When we look at how far she's come, we thank God for the advance knowledge that she would need us both together, fighting and advocating on her behalf and picking up pills from beneath the pillows.

Our sweet son is a teenager now and he's a regular sneakerhead. He likes basketball, rap music and girls, and I make sure he knows how to treat them. He's a straight-A student and an entrepreneur, like his dad and grandpa.

Our oldest son is a young dad, himself, and his love for his daughters shines bright in his eyes, just like M's does when he looks at his children.

Recently, I asked M what his biggest regret in life was, thinking perhaps he'd say that he wished he had lived somewhere more exciting than Rochester, or made bigger investments or spent more time with his children.

But, I was shocked to find that his answer was simply, "I wish I had never cheated on you."

And that was it.

My husband is not the emotional type. But having known him for years, I can interpret that statement to mean, "I am sorry I caused you so much pain. So many years were wasted with you being mad at me. If I had never cheated, we could have been this happy for far more years than we have. And we can never get that time back."

I was totally speechless to find that his biggest regret was that he had cheated on me.

And at that moment, more than ever, I realized the power my forgiveness had held. I realized my perseverance and willingness to move forward had made a life-altering change in my husband's story and it changed our chapters from a momentary marriage to a lifetime love.

And I believe that, if we can do it, you can too. And though you must take your time to grieve, build your self-esteem, get counseling, spruce yourself up, evaluate his level of commitment and willingness to make things work, do take the time to remove bitterness from the equation. Forgive him like God has forgiven you.

He will appreciate your forgiveness in ways he can't quite articulate. And no one will be able to interpret his heart, but you.

When you overcome an affair, it reveals to you a strength you never knew you had. It binds you closer together because you have climbed the insurmountable. You have dodged divorce. You have beaten the odds and outspoken the naysayers. You have grown and matured. You are wiser and more confident. You know that you can rise from whatever knocks you down by working it out together. And you will. Because you made it.

Romans 12:21 says, "Do not be overcome by evil, but overcome evil with good." And John 16:33 says, "I have told you these things, so that in me you may have peace. In this world you will have trouble. But take heart! I have overcome the world." So be encouraged and know that you can overcome this!

If you're working on your marriage, know that you can make it! God honors marriage, and I am a witness that He will bless your efforts. Pray with your spouse and for your spouse and nothing will be able to prevail against you.

And if you don't know God, get to know Him. His office hours are 24/7, He is the greatest of all counselors and His wisdom is free of charge.

And know that if you don't believe in God, He still believes in you! You've tried everything else; why not try God, too?

Pray together to stay together and do it every day! Together YOU CAN MAKE IT!

Dedication

For my handsome M, without whose love and support this book would not exist.

Writing this book has been hard…way harder than I expected.

For a long time, I wanted to share my story with the world. I wanted to help people who have gone through betrayal and are finding it hard to forgive. I wanted them to know that there is hope for their marriage and any relationship worth saving. I wanted them to see that they are stronger than they think and show them they can make it. I wanted to give them wisdom to live by and hope for a brighter day. And I pray I've done that.

Thank you from the depths of my heart for allowing me to tell my truth. I know very few men would allow their wives to put their business in the street the way you have.

Thank you for listening to me read it aloud, in tears, as the painful memories resurfaced. I know that was hard for you. Thank you for praying with me for the souls whose lives will change after reading it and for the brave hearts that will take a chance on making their broken marriages whole again.

There is no measure for how grateful I am that you stuck around, through all of my bitterness, to witness my transformation into a person who forgives. And for not fleeing as I grew into a self-confident woman who stood up, brushed the dirt off and decided to stop being a doormat.

It is an honor and privilege to call you my husband, and I am forever grateful to be your wife.

Love always,
A.

Sovereignty,
by Mercedes DeVine

And when the smoke cleared

She accepted that nothing was in vain

*Her brokenness began to piece together, slowly
she forgave herself*

*When everything that hurt her came to her at
the darkest hour, a light shined*

And she was set free.

References

(In order of appearance)

All bible verses are from the New International Version of the Bible on Bible.com

Stand – Donnie McClurkin, Warner Alliance, 1996

Woman, Thou Art Loosed – T.D. Jakes

The Power of a Praying Wife – Stormie Omartian

Wouldn't Take Nothing for My Journey Now – Maya Angelou

Pathetic, Needy, Insecure Reference – *Sex and the City* – "Cock a Doodle Do!" Season 3, Episode 18

"Until you run out of pages, there's still room to write an epic ending." – Kevin Ngo

"Sovereignty" – Published with the permission of Mercedes DeVine

If you enjoyed this book by April Randolph, you will love her manic but meaningful musings on her blog Lovingmiddleagedlife.

She'd love to meet with you at an event in your area.

Connect with April:
Website: Aprilrandolph.com
Twitter: @aprilwrites1
Instagram: aprilwrites1

Made in the USA
Middletown, DE
26 January 2020